PRAISE FOR INNOVATEHERS

"Thanks to Barbara Kurshan and Kathy Hurley for sharing dozens of stories that provide insight into how women succeed using their own unique power and processes, and how they overcome barriers while maintaining their sense of purpose. A most welcome addition and important read for aspiring entrepreneurs and leaders of any gender!"

—Karen Cator, former President and CEO, Digital Promise

"The future is female—and it's purpose-driven women who will keep the planet safe, habitable, and prosperous for all. Kathy and Bobbi have combined their entrepreneurial spirits to create *InnovateHERs*, a book that every young woman should read. It's the curriculum for the future."

—Tom Vander Ark, CEO, Getting Smart, Author of Difference Making at the Heart of Learning

"Weaving personal narratives with actionable insights, Kurshan and Hurley draw a map of the mindset of women impact entrepreneurs. *InnovateHERs* provides clear direction for women who wish to develop their own entrepreneurial mindset and plot a path to success for their ventures."

—Gillian Muessig, Co-Founder and Managing Director, Mastersfund

"Congratulations to Barbara Kurshan and Kathleen Hurley for writing a much-needed resource that profiles the qualities of women who have succeeded and made a significant contribution to empowerment and inclusion in the business world. I was deeply moved by the amazing stories in this book and could only hope that they would make their way into American schools to inspire a new generation of InnovateHERs."

—Hector Montenegro, Ed.D., President and CEO, MCG LLC, Former Superintendent

"With so much emphasis placed on cultivating the entrepreneurial mindset, it took this book to remind me that this mindset for women and people of color, may be different from the celebrated norm. This book bears witness to character traits that, when hyper-focused on purpose-driven objectives, have the power to change lives and to change the world."

—Angela Nelson, CEO, Stages Learning

"Each life is a journey and every journey expands our minds. By telling stories of how women leaders moved through challenges towards entrepreneurship, Kathy Hurley and Barbara Kurshan provide readers with the opportunity to set their own experiences in context, make greater sense of the world, and progress along their own entrepreneurial paths. *InnovateHERs* provides insight, much to learn from and hope on which to build."

—Gavin Dykes, Programme Director, Education World Forum

"The pandemic demonstrated that inculcating leadership skills is not enough to prepare entrepreneurs to succeed in uncertain, turbulent conditions. *InnovateHERs* highlights the importance of dispositions (tenacity, initiative, resilience) in reaching success. The case studies describe the associated mindsets that enabled these extraordinary women to surmount disruption and thrive on chaos."

—Dr. Chris Dede, Wirth Professor in Learning Technologies, Harvard University

"Through compelling stories of 29 amazing women who have aligned their purpose and passion to succeed in their various fields, Barbara Kurshan and Kathy Hurley bring their research to life on the entrepreneurial mindset. By spotlighting the critical elements that helped each of these women succeed, they illustrate how each of us can develop and foster an entrepreneurial mindset."

—Marissa Wesely, Co-Founder, Win-Win Strategies, Advisor, Women Win

"Barbara Kurshan and Kathy Hurley have written a very insightful and easy-to-read book identifying the mindsets of successful women entrepreneurs who are from diverse professional backgrounds, ages, and cultures. Read it, learn from it, and develop an entrepreneurial mindset of your own."

—Michael Ter-Berg, CEO, Thomson Screening, and Commercial Board at the University of Liverpool

"*InnovateHERs* combines research with women's stories to explain why purpose-driven women rise to the top. Spoiler alert—grit alone won't get you there. There are many factors. But support from others is integral. And that's what these two purpose-driven women are providing with their new book."

—Paula Maylahn, Former SVP
Pearson Education and Principal,
Paula Maylahn Consulting

"The authors of *InnovateHERs* balance the analytical with the anecdotal, giving readers an opportunity to learn through the lessons of an impressive group of InnovateHERs—all with their own distinct stories of business and personal resilience. This book will give aspiring undergrads, business school students, or those who are conjuring up new ventures mid-career validation, inspiration, and most of all reinforcement that anything is possible with the right mindset."

—Evan St. Lifer, CEO, InnovateK12

"Every year, an increasing number of women successfully pave paths to success, despite—and many times in response to—persistent social and economic barriers. This new generation of change-makers; or InnovateHERS, have relied on an entrepreneurial mindset steeped in compassion, interpersonal sensitivity, and a human-centered approach. Their accounts show that the path to the top is unique for every woman and is attainable for those who wish to make a difference in the world."

—Eric and Dori Jones, EdGems Math

INNOVATEHERs

WHY PURPOSE-DRIVEN ENTREPRENEURIAL WOMEN RISE TO THE TOP

BARBARA KURSHAN
AND **KATHY HURLEY**

Written with Laura Smulian

Editing, design, and distribution by Bublish, Inc.

Published by InnovateHERs Press

ISBN: 978-1-647045-35-7 (eBook)
ISBN: 978-1-647045-36-4 (paperback)
ISBN: 978-1-647045-37-1 (hardcover)

Dedications

To my children, Debra and Jonathan, who are my most innovative creations and my most honest advisors. And to my mother, who was a role model and mentor to me and to thousands of young people around the world. (Bobbi)

To my late husband, Charles Blaschke, who always inspired and encouraged me to be purpose-driven in the pursuit of my passions. (Kathy)

CONTENTS

INTRODUCTION

When we set out to write this book, we couldn't have possibly imagined the reception it would get from women and men around the world. From India to San Francisco, we've heard how important it is for our readers to hear the stories of how InnovateHERs have risen to the top. We are grateful to each contributor for openly sharing her journey with us and the world.

If you want to use the book as a tool to spark dialogue in your organization or community, there are three ways to stay involved with our work:

- Book Clubs: Use our book club guide to prompt conversations about the book with employees, clients, and learners.
- Host a Workshop: Invite our team to conduct an in-person or virtual workshop for your organization. Inspired by stories in the book, the workshop dynamics help teams to better understand their entrepreneurial traits and skills.
- Share Your Story: Tell us your story about how you #RoseToTheTop using the "Submit Your Story" link on www. innovateHERs.org for a chance to be featured in our monthly newsletter.

Thank you, again, for reading the book and for spreading the word about the importance of fostering entrepreneurial mindset in women at purpose-driven organizations. If you have any questions about the resources listed above or would like additional information, please contact us at info@innovatehers.org.

Innovate!
Kathy and Bobbi

FOREWORD

Caryl Stern

Executive Director of the Walton Family Foundation

In the mid-1980s, at the ripe age of 28 years old, I was privileged to be named the Dean of Students at a prestigious engineering school. What I did not know, until a newspaper article pointed it out the next day, was that I was the first female Dean the institution had ever had in its 125-year history. With the headline proclaiming, "Sex barrier falls," I found myself being asked to speak to numerous groups of women about exactly how I had managed to break a glass ceiling that, at the time, I was unaware even existed. I wondered what I could say that might be useful, and finding a lack of personal words of wisdom, I interviewed 25 other women leaders I admired, hoping to glean some sort of theme from their experiences. As I did so, I found myself reflecting on my own story in ways that I believe this book will do for all who endeavor to read it.

I understand a great deal of my personal success was gifted to me by what my mother's life had given her. She was a child immigrant. In 1939, in response to the arrival of the Nazis in Vienna, my grandmother was forced to make an unthinkable decision. The only way to ensure the safety of her children was to send them (my mom, aged six, and her brother, aged four) across an ocean to be raised in an orphanage on the Lower East Side of Manhattan. Earlier that same year, the family was forced into helplessness as they watched the world debate the fate of my mother's father, who was a passenger on the MS *St. Louis*—otherwise known as the "Voyage of the Damned." That boat sat in a harbor outside of Cuba for 40 days because no country would accept its refugee passengers.

Both stories were told to me in various forms throughout my childhood and left me with complex emotions. Naturally, my mother was left with emotions of her own, but astoundingly, the main thing she felt was "lucky." She would often tell me she was lucky to have survived and to have had her father survive, but she was also lucky to have had a full life after such a horrific and tragic beginning. In addition to "lucky," she felt an urgent sense of obligation to stand up for what's right and to elevate the voices of the unheard. She became my first role model and mentor—roles she continues to hold to this day.

Unknowingly, my family history contributed in other ways to the entrepreneurial mindset that has served my career so well. I learned the necessities of creativity and thinking outside the box and gained the confidence to employ these skills. They are critical to believing that solutions can be found, even when none are readily apparent. Furthermore, my mother and her father both showed me that resilience can sustain you and propel you forward. These lessons were repeated to me over and over again throughout my time leading UNICEF USA and the years I bore witness to those trapped by humanitarian emergencies.

I have been influenced and taught by many women leaders who have generously lent me their time and their brilliance. Those who stand out to me combine warmth with discipline, confidence with a willingness to continue learning, leadership skills with team membership skills, and humility with pride.

To the many brave women whose shoulders provided the footing for my own career journey, and to those who will provide their shoulders in the future, may this book serve as an inspiration and a tool as you chart your own path and pave a way that others will follow!

CHAPTER 1

Purpose-Driven Entrepreneurial Women

We live in a world driven by innovation. The first-ever vehicle with an engine was invented in 1885, just over 130 years ago—and now, today, through the unwavering push of innovation, emission-free cars are racing down the street without a trace of exhaust. Some are even self-driven. Alexa responds to our needs 24 hours a day, 7 days a week, and the vast majority of the world's wisdom is stored in a hand-sized device that fits inside our pockets. Truly, we live in the golden age of advancement.

Each invention opens new possibilities that invite us to dream bigger and bolder. Five years ago, who would have dreamed we would be able to vaccinate 3 billion people across the world in 8 months against a virus that had never been seen before? Who could have imagined that nearly 30 percent of the workforce in the United States would and could transition to being fully remote?[1] That our kitchen tables would be transformed into full-time classrooms or home offices? Advances in technology, communication, and collaboration have led us to a pivotal moment in which society, more than ever before, has become connected, adaptable, and empowered to work toward a better future.

However, for every problem solved by an invention, another challenge seems to spring up to take its place—and these challenges have only grown more complex and difficult to solve. Climate change and associated crises have companies scrambling to find ways to reduce their carbon footprint. The political climate is more polarized than ever, further widening the wealth gap and creating extra barriers for entrepreneurs to secure important funding for new ideas. Employees are quitting at record levels to transition into jobs with more meaning or flexibility, creating a brain drain and lack of workplace consistency. While new inventions pour out of every corner of the United States, we strongly believe innovation can and must be channeled to improve the world in which we live. Innovation should be a force for good.

All crises seemed to have compounded in 2020. Amid the chaos, we—Kathy and Bobbi—sat down for one of our regular check-ins. We've been close friends for more than 30 years, and then more than ever, we felt the need to connect. After the normal chatter about family, work, and life, we began to open up about what we were seeing in the world. "I just want to make a difference," I said to Kathy, throwing my hands up in the air. "I have been working with entrepreneurs for more than 25 years. I want to take what I have learned and share that with other women. I am not sure how, but I just wish I could help more." Kathy smiled and said, "Well, that's what we do as women. We help." Her comment sat with me for a few days, but I didn't realize the magnitude of what she had said until I came across a quote by the late Fred Rogers: "In times of need, I look for the helpers." Who were the helpers fighting to make a positive change?

That phone call was the first of many in formulating the idea for this book. We realized that there were helpers all around us—and the more we talked about it, the more we came to accept that many helpers were women. They were launching businesses that had social change at the center of their mission, running international nonprofits that were providing essential services during the pandemic, and investing in innovative products and services that sought to build a more equitable world. Women were at the forefront of generating positive solutions in the face of unprecedented challenges.

Throughout our careers, the two of us have been surrounded by women who help one another, their friends, their families, their communities, and the world. And once again, as the world seemed to be spiraling out of control, here we were, watching women do amazing things despite adversity. These women—the helpers—were the inspiration for our deep dive into understanding and painting the Portrait of an InnovateHER.

Finding the InnovateHERs

Our first task was to define an InnovateHER. We could list the impressive women we have worked with over the years one by one, but we struggled to understand the secret sauce that connected them. We witnessed Mary Louise Cohen and Krishanti O'Mara Vignarajah moving mountains to get refugees across the world into safe homes and highly skilled jobs. We heard about the unstoppable Nisha Ligon connecting communities to educational content across the African continent. A call to Lisa Hall revealed she was leading investments in social impact companies at unprecedented rates to extend life-changing opportunities to at-risk communities, and Maia Sharpley was working to do the same in education technology startups. We saw Margaret Huber stepping up to train a new generation of diplomats and Monica Valrani creating early childhood spaces in Dubai to better prepare children for the new world they are to inherit. But what was the common denominator? What made them so remarkable?

After brainstorming a list of the impressive women in our lives, Kathy and I sat down to take a good, hard look at all they had accomplished during the past decade. We landed on a list of InnovateHERs doing exceptional things. Of the final InnovateHERs we interviewed, we count that their work spans five continents with impact in more than 120 different countries. They approach their work in different ways, with 30 percent working at or running startups, 30 percent working at or running nonprofits, 16 percent working in the corporate world, 12 percent leading schools, 8 percent working in professional learning and development, and 4 percent working in the public sector and/or think tanks.

The InnovateHERs are also an incredibly diverse group. An impressive 62 percent are under the age of 50, and 33 percent are primarily based outside of the United States. They bring a rich, ethnic diversity to the table, with 48 percent identifying as non-white. Centering voices from the South Asian, East Asian, Black, Latino, and Middle Eastern communities was important to us—as was discussing the additional barriers these women overcame due to racial injustice and systemic exclusion from equal opportunities. We intentionally included women from a wide range of backgrounds to acknowledge that women of color face additional hurdles when rising to the top of their careers. These women are first-generation immigrants, women who come from families that have faced poverty, and women who are the first in their families to attend college.

As we talked through each of their unique life journeys, we began to look closely at their common traits. I pulled open a study I conducted with a research team at the University of Pennsylvania on the entrepreneurial mindset and leaders in education. I was reminded of the typical profile of an educational leader, based on the results of a survey taken by 124 executive program graduate students who completed the Entrepreneurial Mindset Profile®. In general, these leaders were action-oriented overachievers who used passion as a lever to make a positive impact. They used their entrepreneurial mindset to enact change in their schools, companies, nonprofits, and communities. Could this profile also apply to our InnovateHERs?

The Common Thread: Entrepreneurial Mindset

An *entrepreneurial mindset,* as defined by the researchers of the Entrepreneurial Mindset Profile®, is "the constellation of motives, skills, and thought processes that distinguish entrepreneurs from non-entrepreneurs and that contribute to entrepreneurial success."[2] For the purpose of this book, we have expanded the definition to apply to anyone building or scaling an organization using entrepreneurial traits and skills.

When we contemplate this mindset, we see it describes a certain type of person who acts decisively to create and scale solutions to problems, just like the top-performing women we wanted to better understand. These women are doers, creators, builders, and instigators. They proactively solve problems, propose answers, and build teams that can collaborate to innovate.

The common theme was hard to ignore. The more we talked about it, the more we realized that it was the women who thought creatively and who could adapt to these incredibly trying times—much like entrepreneurs do—that were rising to the top and influencing their respective fields. What's more, they were not doing it in the same way as most men. They were all building toward a purpose or greater cause. If we could figure out how and why they were unified, we knew we had a once-in-a-lifetime opportunity to help future generations replicate the success achieved by these top-performing women.

Interviewing the InnovateHERs

After much debate, we decided to investigate the women on our list using a qualitative approach. We thought this approach would let the conversation flow naturally and let the women share their stories in their own words. We defined our driving questions: What self-identified entrepreneurial traits and skills would these women attribute their success to? Would the results be similar to the research we did on educational leaders at the University of Pennsylvania, or would they differ? And—beyond mindset—how could we uncover the full stories and factors that influenced how these women rose to the top? Was it possible to create a profile for these purpose-driven women?

We decided to speak to all the top-performing women on our list who were remarkably entrepreneurial in their approach to problem-solving and blazing a trail despite adversity, even those who were not entrepreneurs in the traditional sense of the word. Perhaps our biggest challenge in this venture was to understand the intersectionality of the sectors in which these women worked. The organizations they had founded did not fit neatly into one sector or another. Instead, we found that many of these InnovateHERs were merging their own professional journeys with their personal purposes and interests. What do we mean by this?

These women weren't quite educators, though many had an educational lens to their work. They weren't all in public health, though many had experience or built tools that had a real and positive impact on health and well-being. There were government and nonprofit officials who also looked at problems using different lenses. In general, we could say that they were in organizations with social impact, but with the broadening of that expression, it seemed to sell their accomplishments short. These were entrepreneurial women who were out there on the frontlines making a difference on their own terms. They were driven by mission and purpose. Honoring this work required an encompassing expression that would describe the heart these women were putting into innovating solutions to difficult problems.

We scoured the dictionaries for definitions of this kind of work and finally landed on the following definition of a purpose-driven initiative, startup, or organization. A purpose-driven organization has "purpose as its guidepost for decision-making—including the opportunities it decides to pursue and not pursue—to demonstrate commitment to responsible business leadership."[3] Purpose, in this context, grows into something bigger than mere profit or even a corporate social responsibility mission at an otherwise larger organization. Creating a positive impact and serving others should be the *reason* their initiative existed.

With our definitions in hand and our vision clear, what started as just one fateful conversation sparked a year-and-a-half-long investigation. We dove into the world of women leaders, their entrepreneurial mindset, and what most significantly contributed to their professional success. Rather than speculating from the sidelines, Kathy and I set up calls with 27 women we knew and admired. The results form the basis of this book. We also considered it important to tell our stories. Before we tell the InnovateHERs' stories, I want to start by sharing why I, too, identify as an InnovateHER and why these stories are so compelling to me. Kathy will share her story in Chapter 9, as she walks us through how mentorship helped her to gain the skills necessary to rise to the top and why it is important to mentor the next generation of InnovateHERs.

Bobbi Kurshan's Story: The Evolution of an InnovateHER

I love being a teacher! It is often when I am most creative, innovative, and spontaneous. Teaching also provides me with a platform to explore topics about which I am passionate and to ask questions that require disruptive thinking in the classroom. I can expand the term "teacher" to allow me to also serve as a mentor, investor, researcher, and now a storyteller. I have taught middle school, high school, undergraduate computer science, teacher education and professional development, graduate school programs on education and entrepreneurship, and the first-ever corporate training for nurses on the use of digital record keeping. I have even helped corporate managers explore digital transformation. I have also developed games and simulations for learning, mobile apps for teaching refugees, and programs for seniors to become computer literate, and I led the creation of Curriki, a community that that grants teachers access to open education resources and allows them to develop curriculum with open-source design tools.

My story has been driven by the purpose of positively impacting learners. Early in my career, I pursued areas attracting few women, such as mathematics in college and computer science in graduate school. These were learning experiences in conflict. I studied mathematics at a women's college, but I was encouraged to take advanced classes at the coordinate college because they were "more rigorous." While studying computer science at a large, highly regarded university, I decided to concentrate on education and was told by a very well-respected professor that "computers would never be used in schools." I persevered and applied for my qualifying exam with a concentration in education but was told I couldn't take the exam because I had only taken the education courses to bring up my GPA—which was a 4.0. As a result, I was required to add a summer semester to complete additional courses on artificial intelligence before I could take the exam. I was tempted to sue the university but realized that would derail my goal of making a difference. The degree was a means to an end, and I could work hard, take the courses, and keep my 4.0 GPA.

This pattern of challenging the status quo continued when I was hired to lead the department of Academic Computing at an all-women's college where, until I arrived, they had not imagined computer science as a degree or a profession for women. In spite of that, I convinced the CEO of Digital Computing to donate the two VAX computers (two of the first off the assembly line and the newest in mini-computers) to the college. He agreed because it was for women and because I was a woman asking. If you don't ask, you don't receive.

When I left academia, I applied my skills and research to building education technology products. I believed that this work had purpose and impact. My textbook, *Computer Literacy Through Application*, published by Houghton Mifflin in 1986, was used by many schools in the United States and was translated into Russian, Japanese, and Spanish. It impacted millions of young learners—at least 50 percent of whom were women, according to the National Center for Education Statistics. I also designed the first children's products for Microsoft. I seemed to have found my purpose.

This soon led to my third career, as an investment banker. I was thrilled by the challenge of finding and investing in early-stage technology companies that were impacting the future of education. While serving as Co-CEO of Core Learning, the investment fund, I was on the founding team of bigchalk, a large EdTech investment by Core Learning.

As mentors and leaders, women have always been part of my journey. They have helped me see my purpose and have an entrepreneurial mindset. When I left my role as the head of Academic Computing, the president of the college, a woman, told me I was too entrepreneurial for academia. Today, 25 years later, universities are now looking for innovative ways to engage students and survive the pitfalls of transitioning to remote learning. I returned to academia at the University of Pennsylvania as a Senior Fellow and Director of Academic Innovation. Through this role, I have mentored hundreds of entrepreneurs and invested in many companies. I also had the good fortune to meet the CEO of one of the largest online universities in the world, American Public University, and now serve on their public corporate board, APEI.

My journey has included being an academic, a researcher, a product developer, an investor, an entrepreneur and, notably, a woman challenged in a man's world. This book shares these experiences through my story, Kathy's story, and the stories of the InnovateHERs we interviewed.

Why Women?

The decision to tell women's stories was natural both for Kathy and for me. Not only have we had the opportunity to be at the helm of purpose-driven organizations, but we also picked up leadership positions before it was widely seen as acceptable for women to do so. Although we had many men who helped and sponsored us along the way, we were always relieved to find women modelling their own styles of leadership.

We now recognize that many more women are following in our footsteps. In 2019, the percentage of women in senior leadership positions at purpose-driven organizations across the world hit 29 percent,[4] and that percentage has continued to rise, reflecting the upward momentum of women's representation across the public and private sectors. According to a 2015 report from ASU+GSV, 30 percent of education startups are led or were founded by women—nearly twice the percentage in other sectors—and 75 percent have a woman on their executive team. Healthcare and the government/nonprofit sectors follow closely.[5]

Unquestionably, a powerful wave of women leaders is coming. With more women than ever graduating from college and continuing on to master's and doctorate degrees, we project that the future of the workforce will be women.[6] We want them to be prepared with the knowledge that they are more qualified than they know, and we believe that there are skills and traits that will make them more successful in their roles than they ever imagined. Their leadership may look different than traditional models—and that can be a positive thing.

Importantly, as with all leadership roles across sectors, men have traditionally been at the helm of purpose-driven organizations. With a critical influx of women pushing to the top of these organizations as entrepreneurs, directors, CEOs, and board members, we believe a new model of leadership will emerge. We further believe it crucial to examine the driving force behind their rise to the top and how their success is opening pathways for other women to follow. By telling their stories and exploring the traits and skills that helped them to succeed (without replicating a male-inclined leadership style), we hope to inspire the next generation of women to pursue and excel in a purpose-driven field.

Apart from our own personal curiosity, research on women is important for many reasons that have been independently confirmed, as outlined below.

1. Gender-diverse leadership leads to better business results.

Having more women in executive roles benefits the bottom line. Companies with women in at least half of their leadership positions deliver higher sales growth, earnings per share growth, and return on assets, according to a 2016 Credit Suisse report.[7] For example, startups founded and run by women reported higher revenue figures than those run by their male counterparts. In fact, one study by the Boston Consulting Group showed that for every dollar of venture capital funding received, women-led businesses generated 78 cents; for businesses launched by men, the return was 31 cents.[8]

In the world of venture capital, a person or startup achieves *unicorn* status when a privately held startup company has a value (not revenue) of over $1 billion. Historically in the United States, these unicorns have been run by men like Mark Zuckerberg or Elon Musk, who achieved unprecedented investments at a very early age. More recently, men from underrepresented backgrounds such as Byju Raveendran, the founder and CEO of the EdTech company Byju, have also achieved this milestone. Today, women are achieving unicorn status, securing phenomenal amounts of venture capital for their startups.

For example, Guild Education—an online education platform founded by Rachel Carlson and Brittany Stich—achieved unicorn status in November 2019, and in May 2021 the company raised another round of investment, bringing their valuation to $3.75 billion.[9] But that isn't the only example of a recent and highly successful startup led by a female founder. Spring Health, an organization that focuses on eliminating barriers to mental health care, has raised $300 million to date. Its valuation of $2 billion makes its co-founder, April Koh, the youngest woman ever (at the age of 29) to run a unicorn—barely beating out Shippo's CEO, Laura Behrens Wu, for the title.[10] We would be remiss to neglect to mention Whitney Wolfe Herd, the CEO and Founder of Bumble, who was the youngest woman ever to take a company public.[11]

Gender-diverse teams that include and are headed by women do get great returns, and these takeaways also support the notion that women bring enormous intrinsic value to the discussion of leadership.

2. Women lift one another up.

Women-led ventures are more likely to hire women, support women, and promote women across all levels of the company. In short, women-led ventures and teams help other women succeed. Nearly half of consumer service firms with women as founders have women serving in executive roles, compared with only 10 percent of companies started by men.[12] Women's success breeds more success, and as more women make the jump into the C-suite, surely more will follow behind these trailblazers.

Women lift each other up, and their presence in leadership improves business results. This leads to an obvious question: Why aren't more people investing in companies founded or led by women? And if we focus on purpose-driven organizations, wouldn't we want more women to be driving society's most important social impact indicators?

A recent Deloitte and National Venture Capital Association study shows that women comprise only 12 percent of investment partners across the venture capital industry, resulting in a persistent funding gap.[13] We believe that women receive less investment because, even today, they remain greatly outnumbered as investors. If there were more women fund managers, perhaps women would be announcing exciting

IPOs because they received crucial funding in the earlier stages of their startup's existence. While we wait for more women to break the glass ceiling in the investment world, however, we're currently able to see women in positions of power supporting each other in different ways—as with mentorship. This, too, is a crucial way to lift women up. As entrepreneurial leaders, Kathy and I have personally witnessed and benefitted from the power of mentorship and hope to facilitate this connection for women in the future. In Chapter 9, Kathy explains why securing quality mentorship is so important for your career and how to identify great mentors who can support you on your journey to the top.

3. Women engage different skills and traits to be successful.

When Kathy and I were first promoted into leadership roles, it was evident that the positions had been created by and for men. Even with the best intentions, the culture and environment of these organizations pushed us to adopt certain leadership traits that felt inauthentic. For example, we were both similarly pressured to take large financial and budgetary risks in the name of elevating the company's status rather than considering the organization's unique position within the industry and trusting our intuitions. Sometimes we struggled to be heard when voicing our opinions on new initiatives that would break the mold or put a stronger focus on creating social impact. Independent decision-making was saluted, while healthy collaboration was uncomfortable and sometimes perceived as a waste of time. Eventually, it became clear that the expectation of us, as leaders, was to adhere to the conventional thinking promoted by the leadership standards of the time.

This pressure to adjust our leadership skills was not all bad, but it felt strange and sometimes counterproductive to embrace a new approach after having made it so far in our careers leaning on other skills and traits.

Looking back on our journeys through the lens of our research, our discomfort came from being pushed to adopt an entrepreneurial mindset more typical of men in our field—which, as we'll discuss throughout this book, looks quite different from a woman's entrepreneurial mindset. At the time, this discomfort was simply part of stepping into entrepreneurial roles that positioned men at the helm. Women had to adapt to traditionally male skillsets not only to excel but also to be taken seriously. These VP, CEO, or founder positions rewarded traits and skills such as risk-taking, an unemotional and tough-minded approach to hiring and firing employees, and decisive, top-down decision-making that rewarded independence and not interdependence. Deep inside, however, our instincts told us that our collaborative styles, calculated risk-taking, and empathy for our teams were part of what brought us loyalty and excellent results. Internal conflict was constantly present: *Will I come off as too soft? Will they take me seriously if I suggest another way? Do I dare to try something new? Can I push innovative ideas in my own way?*

Our goal to understand the unique combination of traits, skills, and life experiences that make InnovateHERs successful is deeply personal. This curiosity derives from the undeniable fact that women have innate skills and traits that are valuable, making us excellent entrepreneurial leaders. We have seen women excel *and* be empathetic, jumpstart daring new initiatives *within* an established corporate role, and collaborate *across* sectors to leverage the strengths of different organizations. We believe that with the great acceleration of women into executive positions, these skills will move into the limelight.

Why Purpose-Driven Organizations?

Take a moment to think back to your favorite teacher in school or about a medical professional who had a big impact on you when you were sick and in need of care. You shouldn't be surprised if that person was a woman, because research suggests that seven times out of ten times, it was.

Women staff anywhere between 73 and 86 percent of jobs in "helping" industries,[14] like healthcare or education, but those significant percentages have not yet trickled up into leadership roles. Even in 2021, if you were to walk into the boardroom of that same hospital or school, you would be more likely to be greeted by a male leadership majority. Worldwide, only 10 percent of companies of all sorts have women represented at the leadership level.[15] To our dismay, in the United States, those percentages are even lower for women of color and underrepresented populations.

This gap in gender balance in senior leadership positions and in boardrooms is felt acutely by women who have broken through and earned a seat at the table. Many women who sit on corporate boards have the common experience of walking into that same room and being asked to get the coffee or to be the notetaker for the meeting. Although we are beginning to see a change in leadership numbers, it is clear it is not evenly distributed across sectors.

However, a silver lining has emerged over the past decade or so—we have noticed that purpose-driven organizations are evolving more quickly to becoming women-led. A 2018 report by the International Labor Organization showed that in education, over 35 percent of companies worldwide have a woman serving as the CEO, and in human health or social work, 31 percent of companies are led by a woman. Compare this with 18 percent of women-led companies in financial services and 16 percent in construction, and you see a clear picture of the problem.[16] The question is, why does this change appear to be occurring faster in purpose-driven industries?

A 2015 study performed by Imperative shows that women are more likely to be purpose-driven than are men. This likelihood suggests that in the workplace, women prioritize personal fulfillment and providing a service to others more than merely receiving a paycheck.[17] Purpose-driven people are, crucially, *not* subservient—rather, they are more likely to look for roles that integrate their values, lived experiences, and sense of empathy for others.

While it's true that purpose-driven employees can exist in any role—from a supermarket cashier to the CEO of a large nonprofit—the high percentage of women in helping industries suggests a certain preference for industries with social impact. As more and more trail-blazers break through the glass ceiling, we predict that industries that already have a critical mass of women working on the frontlines in the classroom or a clinic will be better poised to place women in top positions in future. Now, if you're like us, when you hear someone say women are more purpose-driven than men, you might raise an eyebrow. Is that a sexist stereotype? Are we sure it isn't an institutionalized bias? Where is the proof?

This question is among the doubts we began to focus on as we sat down with the women we interviewed. In conversational interviews, we hoped to unveil why women seem to be drawn to purpose-driven organizations and whether or not they have an innate purpose-driven approach to their own work and careers. We asked questions like: *Why do you do what you do? What made you become so purpose-driven? What entrepreneurial skills and traits have you leveraged to help you become successful?* We received many answers and found two common themes throughout the stories shared with us, which seemed to point to why women are drawn to this work.

1. Career choices are often inspired by women family members.

Of the 27 women we interviewed, 100 percent could point to a positive woman role model in their life who exemplified working with a purpose. The value of serving others was often instilled in them at a young age, either at home or by an influential adult figure in their lives.

2. Women developed interpersonal sensitivity—empathy—for others after having witnessed or experienced unfairness themselves.

The InnovateHERs' decision to seek out purpose-driven work was often deeply personal and typically linked to having experienced or witnessed discrimination or inequality at a young age. These experiences caused them to develop empathy for others facing similar struggles and influenced the direction they took their career.

Summary of Purpose-Driven Entrepreneurial Women

When we first embarked upon our mission to paint the Portrait of an InnovateHER, our goal was to understand the women around us, reveal what made them so successful, and create a model for future generations that demonstrated how women in purpose-driven roles rise to the top and seek success on their own terms. What we didn't expect was for the stories of these women to touch us so deeply. The interview format we selected allowed these women tell their stories in their own words. We witnessed them sharing moving personal anecdotes about the obstacles they overcame on their path to achieving success. As we interviewed more InnovateHERs, it became apparent that a specific mix of entrepreneurial traits and skills, personal life experiences, and a purpose-driven orientation contributed to their success—enhancing our conviction that women are ideal leaders in organizations aiming to help others.

If you are picking up this book because you are starting out in a purpose-driven career or looking to accelerate your growth in a purpose-driven organization, you're in luck! In these pages, you will find many deeply personal stories that map the path to purpose-driven leadership. If you are reading this because you want to promote more women into leadership roles in your purpose-driven organization, welcome! We hope that these stories provide a compelling case for why women's skills, personality traits, and life experiences uniquely position them to lead purpose-driven organizations. Or perhaps you have a daughter, sister, or niece—a future InnovateHER—that you think could learn from these stories. In that case, we invite you to use this book as a jumping-off point for a rich discussion about how their own life experiences and mindset can prepare them to positively influence the world.

Regardless of why you are here, we hope that anyone who picks up this book will find the same inspiration we did in learning what it takes for women to rise to the top and make a lasting, positive impact in our world.

CHAPTER 2

Portrait of an InnovateHER

Imagine that you *are sitting in a downtown coffee shop buzzing with activity. After many hours of networking and messaging connections on LinkedIn, you've finally secured a highly coveted 15-minute meeting with a legendary CEO of a trailblazing social impact company you've admired for years. You nervously check your watch and flip through your notes one last time. She should be arriving in just a few minutes. You take a few deep breaths to calm the butterflies in your stomach. You've gotten this far, and now you're determined to make a good impression because you may not get another chance. You've been researching her for weeks, trying to figure out smart, insightful questions to ask to secure her mentorship. You're trying to get to one question above all others: What made her so successful? And is it possible to replicate her success?*

Women in top-level positions across all sectors are highly sought after by those looking to understand and perhaps emulate their career pathways. Out of 100 executive leaders in North America, 77 positions will be occupied by men and only 23 by women,[18] dropping to 10 in 100 in a global context. By default, this distribution makes women leaders rare and their time even more scarce. From what we have seen in our careers, successful women take on a few mentees at most, do one or two keynote speeches per year, or occasionally sit down for an interview. As a result, knowledge on how to rise to the top has stayed fragmented and anecdotal.

Instead of needing that hard-to-find mentorship, we hope to speed up the process for our readers. We know that hard work alone is insufficient for success. A 2018 study that surveyed 3,000 professionals at Hive proposes women work 10 percent harder than men. Additionally, women are assigned 55 percent of the work, while men get 45 percent of the load.[19] Clearly, hard work isn't the most important skill needed to reach the C-suite. *By researching what makes an InnovateHER effective in her role, we can now reveal the unique set of entrepreneurial traits, skills, and life experiences that position women to become successful in purpose-driven roles.*

Our interviews with women who work with or have founded purpose-driven organizations grounded our research for this book. However, we added another framework to ensure that our interviews were structured and that the questions we asked would reveal answers about why women rose to the top. Essential to that process was the Entrepreneurial Mindset Profile® (EMP) built by the Leadership Development Institute (LDI) at Eckerd College. Building on the research done by this team, we discovered that entrepreneurial women have four specific personality traits and four specific skill sets that have contributed to their professional success. These come together to form what we call the Portrait of an InnovateHER.

What exactly is the Entrepreneurial Mindset Profile®?

We picked the EMP to do this work because we believe it is the most practical and comprehensive tool on the market for defining and measuring the entrepreneurial mindset. Throughout this book, you will hear us refer to terms such as *entrepreneurial mindset, entrepreneurial personality traits*, and *entrepreneurial skills*. An entrepreneurial mindset, as we established in Chapter 1, can be explained as "a combination of skills and ways of thinking that, when combined, lead a person to have entrepreneurial tendencies."[2] But the research team at the LDI at Eckerd College further breaks it down for us.

The research team hypothesized that certain traits tend to be more deeply engrained in entrepreneurial people, such as the need to achieve and risk acceptance. Similarly, certain skills are prevalent throughout entrepreneurial populations, like persistence and self-confidence. The underlying question, "Are entrepreneurs born or made?" does not yield a satisfying yes-or-no answer. Instead, this research team concluded that entrepreneurial people are both born *and* made.

Entrepreneurial Mindset Profile® (EMP) Scale Definitions

PERSONALITY	SKILLS
Independence The desire to work with a high degree of independence	**Future Focus** The ability to think beyond the immediate situation and plan for the future
Preference for Limited Structure A preference for tasks and situations with little formal structure	**Idea Generation** The ability to generate multiple and novel ideas, and to find multiple approaches for achieving goals.
Nonconformity A preference for acting in unique ways: an interest in being perceived as unique	**Execution** The ability to turn ideas into actionable plans: the ability to implement ideas well
Risk Acceptance A willingness to pursue an idea or a desired goal even when the probability of succeeding is low	**Self-Confidence** The general belief in one's ability to leverage skills and talents to achieve important goals
Action Orientation A tendency to show initiative, make decisions quickly, and feel impatient for results	**Optimism** The ability to maintain a generally positive attitude about various aspects of one's life and the world
Passion A tendency to experience one's work as exciting and enjoyable rather than tedious and draining	**Persistence** The ability to bounce back quickly from disappointment, and to remain persistent in the face of setbacks
Need to Achieve The desire to achieve at a high level	**Interpersonal Sensitivity** A high level of sensitivity to and concern for the well-being of those with whom one works

Credit: Entrepreneurial Mindset Profile® (EMP) developed by Leadership Development Institute at Eckerd College (LDI)

Global Education Entrepreneurship + Innovation   Penn GSE

To reach these conclusions, the research team at the LDI at Eckerd College built an assessment tool to examine different entrepreneurial variables. As shared with us by the EMP research team in February

2022, over 26,800 EMPs have been completed, and the norm group has expanded to 1,047 corporate managers and 1,702 entrepreneurs.

This research has concluded that 14 personality traits and skills define one's entrepreneurial mindset. Seven of these personality traits are more intrinsic, hard-to-change entrepreneurial characteristics, while six are more malleable entrepreneurial skills. The EMP authors chose to include one additional skill, interpersonal sensitivity, as a research point. It was the only variable for which entrepreneurs scored lower than corporate managers. We chose to include it in the book because we believe it is an overlooked skill that is fundamental to understanding purpose-driven, entrepreneurial women.

As the EMP research team administered the assessment, key differences began to appear between people who were drawn into managerial positions versus those who were building new initiatives or organizations. It is now a tool that many corporations and large organizations use to understand and best position the people working on their staff for success. For our purposes, it has helped us to study what entrepreneurial traits and skills are key in leading purpose-driven organizations.

An emerging body of research centers on the importance of the entrepreneurial mindset. We reviewed over 20 different studies that examine this mindset from different angles, use different terminology, and look at distinct traits. We believe that this profile is the best and most well-researched tool on the market, and the traits and skills measured have consistently aligned with our own experiences meeting entrepreneurial people and being entrepreneurial ourselves.

Pam Mayer's Story: The EMP Builder

Perhaps unsurprisingly, the EMP is the brainchild of an entrepreneurial woman. Pam Mayer has the spirit of a coach, which comes across as she greets us with a huge hello and immediately jumps in to pepper us with questions about this book. She loves to understand people and their motivations, and we were no exception—she is curious. Pam is one of the lead researchers on the EMP, and by building this tool, she has helped fill a gap in the market for developing a practical way to show how entrepreneurial mindset compare to corporate mindsets.

After earning her master's and PhD in Educational Psychology and spending many years in education as a superintendent, professor, and department head, Pam transitioned to working in the corporate world as an executive-level coach. She spent more than 15 years working with clients across sectors and continents who were at the top of their game at competitive companies. For a curious person, this was prime research material. Each conversation seemed to reveal something to her, and upon reflection, it seems her investigation into top-level executive minds began informally years before she thought of developing the Entrepreneurial Mindset Profile®.

Throughout the years, and as she gained more experience, Pam noticed a curious trend across companies, countries, and genders in the leaders with whom she worked—the most innovative leaders were discouraged from indulging out-of-the-box thinking. Instead, they were incentivized to tow the company line and do as they were told. This limitation, of course, resulted in deep dissatisfaction, oftentimes leading them to leave their jobs and start their own organizations. So, what kept them at these companies for so long? And were these leaders fundamentally different from their corporate peers?

Pam began to shop around the idea of studying these leaders to different universities and colleges. She had the material but needed to pull together the research team to make it happen. She found a willing partner in Eckerd College. "We need a tool," she announced at her first meeting with the team. "I've taken and delivered a million different assessments. But I can't figure out what makes these leaders different. We need to measure this." Pam recruited Jennifer Hall and Mark Davis to work on the study and do the research. In 2013, they finished researching their findings and built the online survey to offer the public the opportunity to measure their own entrepreneurial mindset. In

2015, the final study was published in *Consulting Psychology Journal: Practice and Research*, and the rest is history.

- The EMP is a tool that measures mindset. In the study "Developing a New Measure of Entrepreneurial Mindset: Reliability, Validity, And Implications for Practitioners" by Mark Davis, Jennifer Hall, and Pamela Mayer,[2] the authors explain the methodology and research-based approach that they used to study entrepreneurial mindset. They break it down into two categories:
- *Entrepreneurial personality traits*, or "the characteristics and motivations that have been found to distinguish entrepreneurs from non-entrepreneurs." This looks at who the person is and why they can do what they do and tends to be "hard-coded" into our personalities—and thus more challenging to change.
- *Entrepreneurial skills*, or "the cognitive and behavioral skills critical to entrepreneurial success." This looks at what a person does and how they do it. With proper training and development, these skills are easier to develop than are personality traits.

When it comes to entrepreneurial women, there are many reasons why they may or may not start their own company or nonprofit. Those reasons normally have more to do with socialization and less to do with mindset. In fact, the women we interviewed who worked for established organizations—like Rebecca Winthrop from the Brookings Institution—chalked up their decision to take on intrapreneurial ventures to external factors like familial responsibilities, financial considerations, and timing. As we move away from a definition that requires "entrepreneurial" people to have a startup, we offer a new framework to think about people with an entrepreneurial mindset. When we refer to entrepreneurial women in this book, we are referring to those who are self-starters, assertive, and driven—those who are on a mission to create a great organization that *does good* and *does well*.

Applying the Entrepreneurial Mindset Profile®
to Our Research

To uncover the Portrait of an InnovateHER, we performed three rounds of research. The first round of research, completed at the University of Pennsylvania, used the Entrepreneurial Mindset Profile® to assess the complexities and variables within the entrepreneurial mindset.

Along with our team at the University of Pennsylvania, Dr. Jennifer Zapf, Dr. Serrano LeGrand, and one of our authors, Dr. Barbara "Bobbi" Kurshan, administered the profile to 124 mid-career graduate students (75 women and 49 men) who work in the teaching, learning, training, and development sector. This sector—one of the largest growing in the purpose-driven economy—provided a small sample of the unique entrepreneurial traits and skills that educational leaders portray. We used these insights to develop our own profile of women drawn to purpose-driven careers.

Our research team then compared the findings to the EMP assessment data, which analyzed individuals' entrepreneurial mindsets across job titles. We found that regardless of job title (e.g., corporate manager, entrepreneur, and education entrepreneur), specific skills and traits emerged that set women apart from men. Additionally, there was a clear distinction between regular entrepreneurs and entrepreneurs with a social or purpose-driven mission.

We then had a list of strengths exhibited by purpose-driven professionals and a hypothesis for which entrepreneurial traits and skills would be portrayed by the women we interviewed. Next, we needed a channel to capture how these women viewed themselves. We developed a self-assessment tool based on the Entrepreneurial Mindset Profile® traits and skills and administered it to the 27 women we interviewed. This tool allowed them to evaluate their own entrepreneurial strengths and weaknesses.

The women who filled out the EMP self-evaluation assessment (see Appendix C) were asked to identify their personal strengths and weaknesses, as well as that of their teams, within the context of the personality traits and skills studied by the EMP. *It is important to note that these women have not taken the formal evaluation, which calculates and portrays a full display of the Entrepreneurial Mindset Profile® traits.* Because this book is based on the intriguing and unique stories these women had to share, we decided to approach their self-analysis using a storytelling format, as we felt this would best capture the nuances of their own opinions and analyze insights that would otherwise go unnoticed by the EMP. This approach provided a way to explore the entrepreneurial mindset of each interviewee and hear, in the InnovateHERs' own words, how it was formed.

After we received their completed self-assessment, Kathy and I conducted individual, one-hour interviews to expand upon our InnovateHERs' answers and truly dig into which skills and traits they attributed to their success. The questions we asked are listed in Appendix B. We also discussed the external factors that had influenced them to start businesses or not, the inspirations for their journeys, and the motivations that kept them moving to innovate for change. These interviews were then coded for keywords in the EMP, and key quotes and insights were pulled out to inform the conclusions and takeaways for this book.

Together, this information led to the creation of the Portrait of an InnovateHER. After compiling the data and analyzing it in depth, we decided to bring these stories to life by writing this book and sharing the inspiring stories through the lens of how an entrepreneurial mindset can help all of us succeed and exceed. The data guides us through examples to understand how embracing entrepreneurial mindsets can help us drive change in even the most bureaucratic of environments. Most importantly, it shows us that an entrepreneurial mindset does not look the same for everyone.

What Makes a Person Entrepreneurial?

When you think of an entrepreneur, what's the first image that springs to mind? You might picture the archetype of a 21st-century entrepreneur, or someone who "organizes and operates a business or businesses, taking on greater than normal financial risks in order to do so."[20] Maybe you think of a young Ivy League graduate with a big vision and little to lose. Maybe you imagine a mid-career manager who is disillusioned by their current job and is excited by what appears to be endless opportunity bubbling up in Silicon Valley, or as someone who has built a multimillion-dollar business out of sheer necessity. Or perhaps, you see a whiz kid who dropped out of school but who codes for hours on end and keeps their finger on the pulse of sectors booming with innovation, disruption, and lots of free-flowing capital.

The first people to come to mind may not be an assistant superintendent who led reforms in her public school district, like Jennifer Ferrari, or a lifetime publishing executive who shifted to the world of art and quilt-making, like Carol Ann Waugh—yet they are incredibly entrepreneurial people. The stereotype of young, idealistic, and technology-laden millennials and Gen Zs as entrepreneurs excludes hundreds of thousands of entrepreneurial-minded workers, many of whom work for companies as employees. What you may not have realized is that entrepreneurial people are all around us, even if they are not launching businesses or nonprofits—yet.

While it is true that some leaders have always self-identified as entrepreneurial, some other leaders develop key entrepreneurial skills throughout their career and life experiences. That is precisely what happened with one of our InnovateHERs, Lisa Schmucki, who spent 30 years in the corporate world at top education publishing and media firms. She spent years developing marketing campaigns and new products. Even though she enjoyed her corporate career, at some point, she started wondering, "Could I be as successful building something of my own?" When social networking took off in 2007, it sparked an idea she couldn't resist. With her years of marketing and business experience and the support of an angel investor, she decided it was the right time to take the risk of starting her own company—a professional social network for the education community, edWeb.net. Since then, edWeb. net has become a groundbreaking professional learning platform for educators around the world. Lisa has created a successful new business model with edWeb.net by providing free professional learning for PreK–12 educators that is supported by the sponsorship of hundreds of leading education organizations.

Lisa Schmucki's Story: Entrepreneurial People Don't Always Start Out as Entrepreneurs

Lisa believes that three key factors allowed her to take the risk to start her own company:

- **Purpose**: Having a compelling idea that gave her a strong sense of purpose. Knowing what she wanted to do and why she wanted to do it.
- **Confidence**: Having many years of experience in building successful new products for companies allowed her to feel that it just might work if she did it on her own.
- **Funding**: Lisa didn't have confidence in her ability to raise money as an older woman starting a business. But the support of an angel investor—who was a former boss and had faith in her work—helped to overcome the funding hurdle.

Even though she hasn't always been a business owner, Lisa has always had an entrepreneurial spirit. For as long as she can remember, she has had a drive to build things and make things better. In elementary school, this drive was reflected in what is now called "project-based learning." In middle and high school, she began taking on leadership roles as the Head of Student Government. Always a changemaker, she proposed a change in the school government from a regular student government to a student-faculty senate—a model that is still in existence today. Lisa has always taken on groundbreaking roles, which led her to become one of the first women to attend Princeton in the class of 1974.

Throughout her career with publishing and media companies, Lisa ran projects to improve systems and results, frequently as part of product development. It wasn't until her mid-career that she started thinking about ideas for her own business, but it took time and reflection to see herself as an "entrepreneur." Her challenges were to believe that she had the ability to succeed and to be willing to take the calculated risk to try.

In our interview, Lisa revealed one of our key takeaways from the research: Women who are driven by passion and empathy often express having low self-confidence when it comes to raising capital to fund their startups. In Lisa's case, she had years of experience in a corporate context and a former boss who was an enthusiastic angel investor and co-founder, which gave her the vote of confidence she needed to take the plunge into entrepreneurship. However, when Lisa's co-founder dropped out after six months, she had to decide whether to continue on her own. That created another crisis in confidence. Her decision to continue came from looking back on all the successful projects she had led in the past. She woke up each day and asked herself, "Do I want to keep doing this today?" Luckily, the answer was always, "Yes."

Lisa's story also confirms an interesting insight from our study: Women tend to be more risk-averse than most men for a variety of reasons. Lisa had a very successful career in publishing and media, so she had less incentive to strike out on her own. When her husband died when their daughter was three years old, she needed to balance her career with her parenting responsibilities. When her daughter graduated from college, she was more willing to take on the risk of leaving the security of a corporate job. At that new stage of life, Lisa was ready to take the risk. But at the same time, she continued to consult on the side for many years for added financial security.

On terms that work for her, Lisa found a way to become the founder of a purpose-driven organization. She has grown edWeb. net with angel investment and by bootstrapping her business model, so she retains equity and maintains control over her vision and the mission of the company. edWeb.net is free and has grown into a community of over a million educators in 185 countries. On this platform, teachers can earn continuing education hours with professional learning edWebinars that are accepted for state teacher license renewal in 43 states.

Her site edWeb.net has grown into a highly trusted brand and community, where educators and sponsors of professional learning at leading companies and non-profits come together to collaborate on all the issues and practices in PreK–12 education. The company has won seven prestigious CODiE Awards for community and professional learning from the Software & Information Industry Association.[21] During the pandemic, edWeb.net grew faster than ever and was able to fill a critical need for online learning and support when educators had to find ways to collaborate virtually and shift their practices.

Lisa's story sets the stage to clear up one of the most common misconceptions about being an entrepreneur. While the traditional definition of an entrepreneur is someone who starts and owns a business, the entrepreneurial mindset goes much deeper than just founding a company. *All successful InnovateHERs know you can be entrepreneurial without starting a business.* We promise! There are many reasons why women do or do not start businesses—we call them *InhibitHERs*, or the things that hold women back from success. In Chapters 7 and 8, we will talk about how these internal and external factors influence women's careers and how they can be leveraged for success.

For now, remember this: We are surrounded by entrepreneurial people all the time, with or without the title of CEO or Founder. These people are heading up departments at growing companies or leading important initiatives within nonprofits, governments, schools, hospitals, and corporations. Understanding what makes them tick and what skills make them successful can help you learn how to build more effective teams, better delegate responsibilities, and leverage strengths to find success and rise to the top at any point in your career, regardless of whether you start a business or not.

Introducing the InnovateHER

You may have read about her in a recent *Fast Company* or *Inc. Magazine* article or caught her profile in the *Forbes 30 Under 30* list. She might be the speaker you saw at a university commencement or the recipient of a prestigious award at an industry-wide conference. She is driven by a love of what she does and has a deep determination that has helped her advance to the top of her field. ***An InnovateHER is a woman who uses entrepreneurial skills and traits to create a positive impact while achieving a greater personal purpose.*** The combination of these skills and traits is what makes her so powerful, unique, and effective in her role. She strikes a balance that allows her to do the work she loves on her terms.

When we refer to the Portrait of an InnovateHER, we are referencing the precise combination of entrepreneurial personality traits and skills—her entrepreneurial mindset—that enable her to successfully lead purpose-driven organizations. These specific traits and skills, inspired by the EMP,[2] show a unique entrepreneurial mindset that looks different from a man's profile. The Portrait of an InnovateHER also highlights certain characteristics that are more pronounced in women who choose to start new initiatives in the social-impact space. An InnovateHER shows the following entrepreneurial traits:

- *Driven by passion—but not necessarily passion for one thing.* For an InnovateHER, passion is built into how she experiences life. She looks at work as exciting, rather than tedious or draining. Even on the dull days, InnovateHERs find fuel in the small things that keep them moving to advance the work they love. InnovateHERs *live* with passion—they don't *find* it, which is why passion is listed as a personality trait and not a specific topic or area of interest.
- *Shows an intense need to achieve.* InnovateHERs aim for the top—the very, very top. Their desire to reach the loftiest goals, receive recognition, and achieve at a high-level span across

the board. Usually, the need to achieve shows up early in life, manifesting as strong grades, the tendency to take on lots of responsibility, or the proclivity for competitiveness.

- *A calculated risk-taker.* When put in the context of the entrepreneurial mindset, risk is a going after things you want, even if you aren't sure you are going to get them. For an InnovateHER, that willingness is constantly balanced by other factors like the impact on her team, family, or loved ones. You might find her presenting ambitious strategic plans that delight investors but are, at the same time, realistic and achievable for the team.

- *A bias to action.* The InnovateHER is not a woman who likes to wait for the perfect moment to act. She tends to show initiative, make decisions, and feel impatient for results. This bias to action for InnovateHERs often manifests as launching new programs, products, or businesses. Rather than waiting for someone else to solve things for her, she is willing and able to get the job done herself.

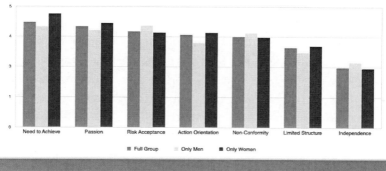

Purpose-Driven Leaders EMP Result – Personality Traits Only

The InnovateHER has also built more entrepreneurial skills over the course of her life to compensate for the fact that men tend to exhibit more entrepreneurial personality traits. To keep up, she has evolved. Some of her hard-earned entrepreneurial superpowers include the following:

- *Persistence.* This is a woman who bounces back from disappointment—time after time after time. She keeps moving in the face of adversity and does not give up even when the odds are stacked against her. In excess, she might be blindsided by her determination to make her vision a reality.
- *Optimism.* To create, one must keep a positive attitude about various aspects of one's life and the world. Even in a remarkably challenging year, the women we interviewed spoke positively about the future and expressed an outlook that reflected an optimistic worldview.
- *Idea generation and execution. Idea generation*, or the ability to see and brainstorm multiple ways to reach important goals, is not enough to describe an InnovateHER alone. Rather, this combination is accompanied by *execution*, or simply put, the ability to get the job done. An InnovateHER is both a dreamer and a doer. She exists comfortably in the space between these two skills.
- *Interpersonal sensitivity.* Our interviews confirmed that *interpersonal sensitivity*—or an attention to the well-being for others—is a superpower for purpose-driven women. Even though entrepreneurs score lower than corporate managers on this skill in the EMP, our research confirmed that the InnovateHER ranks highly on interpersonal sensitivity, setting them apart from the typical entrepreneurial leader. Throughout the text, you may also see this skill referred to as *empathy*[22]—"the ability to understand and share the feelings of another"—which reflects how the women interviewed referred to this skill in their own words.

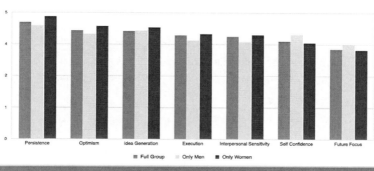

If we were to put all the mindset traits in a machine and ask it to create the perfect InnovateHER, no one woman would ever represent 100 percent of each of the entrepreneurial traits and skills. InnovateHERs can have any combination of those skills and exhibit them to varying degrees of intensity. If we think about this as a recipe, these traits and skills would be the ingredients. Too much of one skill or trait might overpower the others, while too little might mean the recipe doesn't work. When it comes to the proportions, certain combinations work better than others. It is then up to the chef to find the right balance to be successful.

Needless to say, the intensity of each of these traits and skills falls on a continuum for each InnovateHER. Perhaps the tricky part to wrap our brains around is that there is no one "right" answer or formula for becoming a successful InnovateHER. However, what we did find in the research is that there are potent combinations that are especially powerful. So, what do the most effective combinations look like?

Lisa Hall's Story: Doing Well and Doing Good

Lisa Hall, the Impact Chair of Apollo Global Management, was born in a city of contradictions—Baltimore.

"Baltimore is home to me. It's unique," she said with a smile and a sigh. "It's a city that has two sides. On one hand, it's a working-class, real salt-of-the-earth population that works hard and lives frugally. And on the other hand, it has extraordinary wealth. I believe growing up in Baltimore was fundamental to my success because I was able to see contradictions and develop a real sense of what the world was like on both sides of the coin."

Lisa's exposure to different socioeconomic realities from a young age deeply influenced her philosophy on life. She witnessed the development of Baltimore alongside the people who were displaced. She saw the city transform, go through growing pains, and grow into a tourist destination. That experience showed her how fragile life could be and how quickly one's circumstances could change. She herself grew up in a working-class family. Her mother was a Home Economics high school teacher for 30 years and later a diversity coordinator for a private school. Her father was a social worker for school and healthcare systems. They both grounded Lisa in a sense of duty and higher order from a young age. "The ultimate success," her father would say, "is serving others." Though they never pushed her in one direction or the other, they always gently reminded her that to be successful, she had to lift others up alongside her. But finding the balance between *doing good* and *doing well* was not easy.

Lisa made the decision to *do well* when she went to the University of Pennsylvania as a Wharton undergraduate. Following graduation, she fatefully—and accidentally—ended up in a credit training program at a large bank and eventually worked in the group that made loans to affordable housing developers. "I hit the jackpot for a first job. Here was this work that made money, was business-oriented, finance-oriented, *and* served the common good, because it produced affordable housing. And I had a series of jobs along the way that really did that." Without planning it, she had found work that allowed her to *do well* and *do good*, honoring the values instilled in her at a young age. Even when she attended Harvard Business School a few years later, she knew she wanted to do more than just finance and real estate development. She knew she wanted to have a social and environmental impact.

After several years of working in real estate, a colleague suggested that she investigate impact investing, at the time known as *community investing*. They connected her to a contact at Calvert Foundation, now known as Calvert Impact Capital, a pioneer in the impact investing space. The organization introduced her to an established way of *doing good* and *doing well*. She jumped at the chance to be on the cutting edge of what it meant to invest in businesses that were purpose-driven and making a profit. She could make money while also making a difference. Without questioning it, she took on a role at Calvert that ultimately led to her leading the organization as President and CEO. Today, she is recognized as one of the pioneering thought leaders in impact investing and serves as an advisor to one of the world's largest alternative asset managers.

Even though Lisa has grown as a professional and continues to have experiences that are informed by values developed in her childhood, she shares that it has not been easy. One of the most challenging aspects of her career has been feeling like she can't fail, so her resume has become her safety net. "The problem is," she explained, "there are not a lot of people who came before us who look like me. There wasn't anyone who I could really look up to in business. In many ways, I raised myself in the business world." When talking about business school, especially, she described how the attention to status, educational attainment, and belief systems were far from her own.

Walking the tightrope between these two worlds meant understanding how the other world worked, too—without letting it consume her. It meant having to work twice as hard to make the same connections, to get her foot in the door, and to relate with the people who were around her. In the most difficult times, Lisa leaned into her purpose and used hard work and doing her best as a shield of protection when the "going got tough" on her path to becoming an InnovateHER. Her story exemplifies two crucial maxims for InnovateHERs:

1. Work to achieve your greater purpose by embracing a long-term vision.
2. Give your purpose time to mature. You can refine your instilled values, gain experience, and update your own goals to create or find a perfect job for yourself.

There are many things that money can buy, but values are not one of them. Lisa's values played an important role in protecting her throughout all the environments she had to pass through to get to where she is today. They kept her on the path to achieving the blend of *doing well* and *doing good,* and the combination of the two has led to her reputation as one of the top impact investors in the United States today. Her path to becoming an InnovateHER was set from a young age, but it was the skills she picked up along the way and the clarification of her purpose that made her truly stand out in her career.

InnovateHERs: How Traits and Skills Complement Each Other

"Do you think you were born to lead, or did you build the skills along the way?" By asking our interviewees this question directly, we were able to hear from the InnovateHERs themselves as to whether they thought their entrepreneurial mindset was coded into them at a young age or was rather a learned set of skills based on environmental influences, role models, and social factors. Could we finally answer why it is that many great leaders demonstrate entrepreneurial characteristics from a young age? Or is the concept of a "born leader" actually a myth perpetuated by those with fixed mindsets?

Most researchers who have investigated this question will give you a long-winded answer to these questions, but to save you time, we'll give you a preview of what the InnovateHERs thought: **Leaders with**

an entrepreneurial mindset are both born *and* made. This aligned with both our research and the team behind the EMP's work. Our subsequent studies reveal that the skills necessary to succeed are even more nuanced for those who are drawn to purpose-driven organizations and work. These skills go beyond just typical entrepreneurial mindset traits because it takes a special kind of leader to build new initiatives and ventures in mission-driven sectors that are traditionally under-resourced and have more red tape.

It takes an InnovateHER to get the job done.

In the following chapters, we'll explore the intersection of entrepreneurial personality traits and skills by telling the stories of successful women who leveraged a combination of both to have an impact. These stories will illustrate how these traits and skills combine to create greater impact, highlighting the following facts:

1. Passion was the number one self-reported personality trait. This isn't surprising—we did interview purpose-driven women, after all, who are incredibly passionate people. What the research did reveal was that those who were passionate and who scored below a 3 or a 5 on entrepreneurial skill sets were not in positions of leadership. In Chapter 3, we will highlight that those who excelled in their positions were the ones who led with passion combined with persistence and interpersonal sensitivity. Take Anjlee Prakash, the founder of the Learning Links Foundation in India, who took *20 years* to convert her dream of bringing cutting-edge learning technology to India into a reality by building a team of 1,200 people to work with 45,000 schools across India. Her remarkable persistence has facilitated learning for millions of people by providing educators and learners with the latest learning technology while, at the same time preparing students for jobs in emerging sectors. Another example is Zoë Timms, who let her empathy for

others help her assimilate into a completely different culture on the other side of the world and build a community-led organization leading holistic public health and educational initiatives for women across India. To become a successful InnovateHER, you will need empathy to create a product or service that adequately addresses a pain point for your customers or users. Empathy, combined with, passion and persistence, will help you to see your vision through to the end.

2. The need to achieve was the silent, yet omnipresent, trait among the founders and CEOs we interviewed. In Chapter 4 we'll examine why, although it was rarely self-reported, the need to achieve is one of the most important personality traits for an InnovateHER—if not the most important. Through our interviews, it became clear that like Lisa Hall, InnovateHERs highly valued doing well *and* doing good at the same time. It also revealed that there are two skills that help high achievers to make an impact. The first is the persistence to never give up when failure presents itself—shown by Sabari Raja's vision to create a better world through connecting students to real-world experiences. The second is a combination of idea generation and execution, or the ability to be able to dream big and make things happen. As an example, we'll look to Nisha Ligon, who dreamed of making learning fun and enjoyable for kids across the African continent—and then built the skill sets to make this dream a reality.

3. Calculated risk-taking is a trait that differentiates women from men. For women, risk-taking is a complicated calculation due to many social and cultural factors, but we repeatedly saw a theme of two skills that helped women take risks at purpose-driven organizations: optimism and interpersonal sensitivity. In Chapter 5, we will look at why, to take a risk, you must be optimistic—like Sherrie Westin, who helped to navigate one of the most ambitious cross-sector partnerships in the nonprofit world to get refugees vital information via

Sesame Street's platform. Focusing on what is possible instead of on what stands to be lost helped her lead teams that built effective coalitions across borders, industries, and time zones. Successful InnovateHERs also proved that having a strong "why" for risk-taking can help motivate those who are more driven by empathy. Empathy helps InnovateHERs to build a better impact-driven product—as demonstrated by Vicky Colbert, whose empathy for teachers in rural Colombia led her to completely disrupt the educational model not only in Latin America but also in developing countries across the world.

4. Action orientation is one of the most exciting personality traits in the entrepreneurial mindset. Highly valued by investors, it is a golden ticket to success in the initial stages of starting a new initiative or venture. In Chapter 6, we address the crucial role of action orientation in getting an organization off the ground. We follow the stories of Katie Fang and Ana Hidalgo in their respective efforts to attract clients, financial resources, and team members to launch companies with social impact. Katie Fang shows how, when combined with idea generation and execution, this trait can lead to the coveted "hockey stick" growth curve for a business—meaning millions of dollars in revenue in just a few years. Ana's story shows how, even amid a crisis, her optimism allowed her to create a new school model and advocacy organization that allows more children to learn in non-traditional classroom settings.

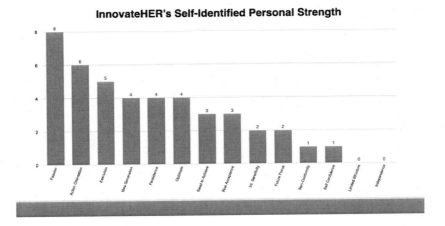

InnovateHER's Self-Identified Personal Strength

Ultimately, the entrepreneurial mindset is a powerful lens for examining how women are uniquely positioned to create an impact, despite a variety of gender-specific barriers. Their traits and skills help them to look at problems creatively and bring previously overlooked approaches to the table. Because purpose-driven organizations often live within an under-resourced sector filled with enormous barriers, we can learn from the InnovateHERs who have embraced and built out the most entrepreneurial parts of their personalities to build and grow organizations with massive impact across the globe.

Summary of the Portrait of an InnovateHER

All of us have entrepreneurial personality traits and skills. Some traits have been hard-coded into us at an early age and strengthened as we pass through different trials and phases of our education and careers. Some of us have very weak entrepreneurial traits but have strong skills and diverse teams that help us achieve our goals. These skills and traits can be gifts, if we learn what they are and how they impact our work. Discovering your strengths and focusing on how to leverage them can help you become more self-aware and effective in your career path and in your role as a purpose-driven leader. They can also help you get to the next level in your career. Understanding the formula for calculated risk, channeling your passion, harnessing the need to achieve, and leveraging action orientation are powerful steps toward advancing and achieving your professional goals.

Learning what skills help InnovateHERs become effective can lead you to have a greater impact in your organization and to success. Though our InnovateHERs come from different parts of the world and walks of life, the skills they have built have been crucial in helping them to start and run corporations, startups, and nonprofits or run successful programs at large purpose-driven organizations. Learning to build new skills to balance out their innate traits has helped them to attract funding, build programs, grow teams, and make a positive impact on their communities. Their paths have not always been straightforward, and there have been many challenges along the way, but they ultimately reveal one important truth: There is no one right way to be a changemaker but leaning into your unique entrepreneurial mindset and finding the formula that works for you can help you navigate tricky or ambiguous waters on the pathway to success.

Our findings raise additional questions about the external factors that may influence an InnovateHER's career pathway. Chapters 7, 8, and 9 will address questions such as the following: What role did socialization play in the fact that women seem to portray fewer entrepreneurial personality traits than men? Do women become more entrepreneurial with mentorship during their careers, or is it more powerful to have examples of women entrepreneurs at home? Why does self-confidence seem to be the Achilles' heel for women, and how does that play into a lower tolerance for risk or a higher need to achieve? All these questions will help us finish painting the Portrait of an InnovateHER to show who flourishes in purpose-driven organizations—and why.

CHAPTER 3

Passion + Empathy + Persistence

Passion, or "the tendency to experience one's work as exciting and enjoyable rather than tedious and draining,"[2] was hands-down the most universally mentioned and openly agreed upon essential InnovateHER trait. It is not the same thing as *purpose*, which is a specific topic or direction that passion can be aimed in. Passion is the fuel that feeds the flame and is what keeps people going despite struggles or setbacks. In the EMP, it is cited as a personality trait that you are born with. Passionate people don't always have a purpose, but purpose-driven people almost always have passion as an entrepreneurial personality trait. If you look at organizations making meaningful change, you usually won't find passionate people far behind.

But what if you haven't found "a passion" yet? This is where the entrepreneurial mindset distinguishes between passion as a personality trait and passion as a hobby. Passion is not necessarily about one specific thing or pastime but is rather an approach to life. As you might recall, entrepreneurial personality traits are built into us from early on. Do you get easily excited about new ideas, or are you quick to dive into new projects? If that sounds like you, then you might rank high on the passion scale.

Almost unanimously, the women we interviewed agreed that being passionate and approaching your work with zeal is a prerequisite for leading transformational initiatives in a purpose-driven organization. Apart from being a trait that women who had founded their own organizations most identified with, we also saw it deeply ingrained in intrapreneurial leaders as well. *Intrapreneurs*, or people who lead internal programs at large organizations, are often just as passionate as people who start their own ventures. It is evident in all they do. The long hours, the excited hand gestures, the moving speeches, and the ability to persuade others to believe in what they do are all hints that you might be in the presence of passion.

This shouldn't come as a surprise to anyone who has worked for a great cause. In industries like healthcare, education, or in local government, there are chronic shortages of resources, significant bureaucracy, and an epidemic of being overworked. Diving into work that is often riddled with obstacles and that has no guarantee of paying off demands the sort of person who will be motivated and excited to show up on a daily basis—someone who leans on passion as a personality trait to overcome these daunting barriers. Despite these difficulties, both education and healthcare startups tie for the most stable industries in which to start a business. In large part, that status is thanks to the passionate people behind the scenes who refuse to give up.

Hiring people who are passionate is crucial for anyone doing purpose-driven work because passion drives change. A 2015 study by

Imperative revealed that 28 percent of the United States workforce considers themselves purpose-driven.[17] These team members tend to stay for more than two years, are more fulfilled on the job, and are more likely to feel deeply about the impact their work is having. Overall, this leads to greater fulfillment and engagement on the employee's side. We believe these individuals—who love what they do and who find joy in the daily challenges of their job—would rank highly in passion on the EMP. They are also the sort of people uniquely suited for purpose-driven work that not only aims to make a positive social impact in the world but also generates a financial return.

The women we spoke to were not afraid to share how their tendency to approach their work with passion showed up in their organizations and united their teams. They use passion to drive difficult-to-capture research, build personal connections with end users, and add value to people who come from different backgrounds. Though passion alone isn't enough to drive an organization's growth—very few single factors are—it was the magic trait that was woven through all the organizations we researched. The verdict is in: Leading with passion is essential for starting and scaling new initiatives. The big question is: How does it combine with entrepreneurial skills?

Zoë Timm's Story: A Journey to Social Justice

Portrait of an InnovateHER: Passion + Interpersonal Sensitivity

Some people will chase a dream for their whole life with a clear goal in mind. As for others, a dream opportunity might fall right into their laps when they least expect it. Zoë Timms falls into the latter category. Twenty-five years ago, Zoë was one of five hundred daydreaming students in a South Asian studies lecture at the University of Wisconsin-Madison. Hoping to catch the attention of the students, the professor casually mentioned that he would be opening spots for UW's Year-in-India and asked whether anyone was interested.

Zoë was surprised to find her hand waving in the air. One year later, she was sitting in a classroom in Hyderabad learning Telugu with seven other intrepid students. The program was designed so that each student would complete an independent study, write a thesis, and then return home. But one thing led to another, and what was supposed to be a yearlong trip turned into an 18-year journey that continues to this day. Zoë's adventure had begun.

Her initial study focused on measuring the environmental impact and the history of a local river on small farm owners. Initially, the task was daunting. Writing the paper for school required interviewing lots of farmers, which meant gaining fluency in the language and culture. As her language skills improved, she began to fall in love with the stories she heard from the farmers and their families. She knew in her heart that one year wasn't enough time. Zoë went back to Wisconsin to complete her final semester, and after graduating, she returned to India to manage the University of Wisconsin's study abroad program in Madurai.

During her time working for the University, Zoë met a young woman who she "could just tell was smart—she spoke five languages, worked a side-job, and shared with me that she dreamed of getting an MBA." Zoë figured she came from a middle-class family and had the support of her parents since she was so accomplished. But one day, she invited Zoë home to have lunch with her. "We passed through the nicer neighborhoods, and slowly, the houses became simpler, more crowded, and finally our taxi dropped us off at a small two-roomed home. When we walked in, her father was passed out—drunk. In the next room, her mother was sitting on the floor. Due to leprosy, she was unable to stand. My perspective shifted—this young woman was supporting her whole family, and she had no safety net whatsoever."

It would have been easy to chalk this young woman up as another statistic of poverty, but Zoë did not look away. Instead, determined to help her reach her goal of getting an MBA, Zoë leveraged her network to fundraise a few thousand dollars for a scholarship to a local MBA program. The campaign was a success; the young woman was off to school! But the work was far from being done.

In this process, Zoë had met many other young women in India who were bright, talented, and ambitious but lacked the funds to pay for their education. There was so much need, and she realized her newly acquired skills of cultural immersion and empathetic leadership were informing her vision of creating a community-centric development model. Her passion was shining through, but she found the secret to opening doors and connecting with others was through her ability to empathize while leveraging personal, human connections. As she worked to support these young women, others began to ask, "How can we help, too?"

To address the scale of need, Zoë formed the Women's Education Project (WEP) to support young women's educational goals. Without institutional support from foundations or corporations at the beginning, Zoë understood the power of storytelling, using heart, passion, and empathy to connect to donors. Additionally, her nonprofit model was simple: Find a woman who needed a scholarship, connect her to a local support system, and fund her education. However, as the project grew and she got to know more young women, it became clear that there were more barriers to getting an education than just money. Nutrition, language, familial dynamics, and health education were all involved. Getting these young women to graduation was more complex than just paying for school. Zoë also knew that to best support the girls, a safe space would be needed to meet and learn side by side with friends. As many more students began to attend the WEP center, she identified the need for local community leaders to implement solutions beyond scholarships.

She made the decision to hire three women who had been born and raised in local communities to support the program's rollout in three different cities. She created a template that could be used to connect the young women to local support systems while attending courses at the center. To do this, she utilized a "sisterhood approach" that provides spaces for young women to learn together and from one another on their education journey. Each center has the discretion to adapt the program to the needs of the young women in their areas.

Throughout the years, many people challenged the holistic approach taken by the Women's Education Project and suggested that it would be better to focus on one issue at a time by creating either a computer literacy program or a nutrition program. They said the holistic and individualized approach wasn't scalable. But Zoë stuck to what she was seeing on the ground, and holistic, empathy-led solutions driven by local leaders intimately aware of the students' needs and community opportunities simply worked. In 2020, working closely with WEP program directors, students, and alumnae, Zoë revised the program, incorporating 19 years of local program offerings to form the WEP Leadership Academy. To date, WEP has helped over 2,500 girls become economically independent.

For Zoë, what started as a personal project to help one young woman cascaded into a larger movement that enabled thousands of girls and young women to transition to economic freedom by connecting them to education and training programs. Driven by a passion for locally led solutions and a mission to build a flexible program centered on compassion and empathy, Zoë has built a program that is poised to expand its positive impact on young women throughout India. Zoë's own mix of passion and interpersonal sensitivity helped her adapt to the local culture and build a truly community-centered development model.

Passion and the Role of Empathy

While it was abundantly clear that passion is a prerequisite for purpose-driven work, our research at the University of Pennsylvania also revealed a fascinating insight: Women have a leg up on men in interpersonal sensitivity as a skill. We were itching to ask the women about it in our interviews. Did they feel that their empathy for others was a defining leadership characteristic, or was that a stereotype that was no longer relevant?

Using the definition of the EMP, *interpersonal sensitivity* is "a high level of sensitivity to and concern for the well-being of those with whom one works."[2] As a reminder from Chapter 2, for the purpose of this book, we use this term interchangeably with *empathy*, defined as "the ability to understand and share the feelings of another."[22]

The EMP research reveals that entrepreneurial individuals have traditionally scored low on the empathy scale. Yet time and time again, we heard from our interviewees that this skill is a crucial ingredient in the secret sauce of success for InnovateHERs in purpose-driven work. Passion was clearly a lifelong motivator for Zoë and a huge factor in why she chose to work two jobs and kept going for 18 years despite numerous challenges. But in Zoë's case, she found her true purpose and scaled her organization using empathy to connect with her team. Her extraordinary interpersonal sensitivity set her apart and led her to build a locally based solution that kept the people she aimed to serve at the center of her model. Using her entrepreneurial personality trait (passion) and her skill (interpersonal sensitivity) developed over time, she created a model that attracted donors from around the world to support her organization.

A telltale sign of a leader who ranks high on passion and interpersonal sensitivity is something we think of as "resource magnetism," or being able to attract funding or in-kind support for a mission—and it's clear that Zoë falls into this category. Zoë attracted donors by sharing the stories of the girls she was working with. Passionate leaders connect people to their ideas, businesses, and initiatives simply because their energy is contagious, but empathetic people lead with heart. You can't help but be excited when you're around them; you want to be part of whatever it is that they are starting because you know it's grounded in a genuine interest in the well-being of others. This combination of interpersonal sensitivity and passion can be a powerful incentive to drive investment, team building, and traction in purpose-driven organizations.

The results from Eckerd College's use of the EMP reveal that passion was ranked the second highest personality trait in the 2020 combined group of 18,721 people. That means that in both corporate and entrepreneurial leaders, passion was a significant factor in defining an entrepreneurial mindset. Additionally, women scored significantly higher on interpersonal sensitivity than men did. Our research at the University of Pennsylvania reinforced these results.

Though we can interpret these results in different ways, in our conversations with women in leadership positions, passion was mentioned over 250 times, which makes it by far the most discussed trait or skill on the EMP scale. The InnovateHERs often discussed passion as a strength that they rely on when driving a vision forward and convincing stakeholders to get behind their ideas—more so than prior experience or an appeal to logic. Then, they engaged interpersonal sensitivity to get their team's buy-in and loyalty. By building people-centric organizations, they generated strong growth and achieved a positive impact in collaboration with others.

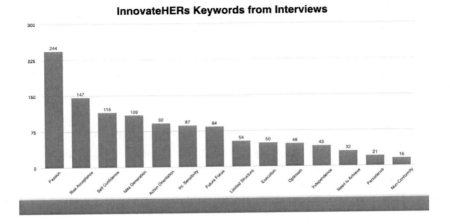

Passion is an indispensable InnovateHER trait, and interpersonal sensitivity, or empathy, is the secret sauce to humanize lofty ideas to connect with people. Those who had their own businesses referred to their passion as the reason they knew it would be safe to branch out on their own and create their own initiatives. When combined with persistence, passion was also what kept them going during challenging times. Approaching their work passionately was a strategic differentiator and allowed them to stand out in the crowd when raising funds, advocating for new initiatives, or implementing a new project. This approach hits close to home for us as authors, too—passion is why we found ourselves studying the entrepreneurial mindset and writing this book, interpersonal sensitivity is what allowed us to connect with the InnovateHERs, and persistence is what led us to publish these stories and research!

Anjlee Prakash's Story: Scaling a Purpose-Driven Organization

Portrait of an InnovateHER: Passion + Persistence

Once an organization is successful, it is common for most entrepreneurs to break with co-founders or leave their companies to pursue new interests and ideas. The average time an employee spends at any job is four years, and so when Anjlee Prakash casually mentioned that the majority of her founding team has stayed on board for the past 18 years, it was immediately clear that her organization is extraordinarily unique. The success of Learning Links Foundation is undeniable: 1.8 million students, 2.2 million teachers, and 6.8 million community youth and adults impacted with a team of over 1,000 employees. What is the secret to their success?

Before we answer that question, let's back up a little bit. Though she always knew education was her calling—she got both a master's and a PhD in education—Anjlee spent years in the private sector before taking the leap of faith to start her own nonprofit. She showed up to perform her corporate role every day, determined to lead her teams in a way that promoted purpose and also achieved results, but this work still wasn't fulfilling her dream of having an impact on those in need. She *knew* she wanted to do something that was more meaningful to her. Finally, a combination of feeling unfulfilled in the corporate sector and having faith that she had the skills to make real changes in the education ecosystem led her to quit her job to start Learning Links Foundation. Once she made that commitment, she said, "I never looked back."

"The goal was simple," Anjlee said in her interview. "We wanted to give opportunities to teachers and students across the country. We believed in access to good quality education so that students could become what they dreamed of being. We aimed to make learning come alive for students, so it wasn't a onetime thing but rather a passion that they followed throughout their whole lives."

Anjlee knew immediately that a one-size-fits-all education model would not work for India. The incredible diversity within the country meant that it would be essential to get down to the local level to understand the unique challenges of the community at hand. This wasn't a surface-level issue; it was one that couldn't be resolved without digging deeper into the problem. "To be successful in providing well-designed and need-aligned learning experiences, I knew I needed to start with teachers, as I believe they are central to all change," Anjlee shared. "It boils down to strengthening the source—training those who impart learning to others." She recruited a small team of like-minded folks who shared a similar philosophy, and together they took on their first project of training 10,000 teachers in technology-enabled education across three different locations in India. The initiative grew rapidly and created a place for Learning Links Foundation as a leader in learning and professional development in the country.

It takes a special kind of leadership team to reliably deliver the best. People began to take notice, and without a marketing team, word of mouth began to spread about this group of passionate educators who were transforming learning. As the Learning Links Foundation's early-stage team went from community to community to investigate local challenges, they slowly began to build a strong network with the state governments. The core team all shared the same strategy: Create systemic change from within by working with the government and communities—don't create parallel systems.

The government bodies and communities responded. The number of teachers trained and schools transformed continued to grow rapidly, even without a marketing strategy. Simply put, the Learning Links Foundation's collaborative approach to bringing sustainable change was a success. The fact that the team showed positive and consistent outcomes in projects taken up across the country spoke volumes about their commitment. The results were evidence that what they were doing—and how they were doing it—*worked*. Next, the team decided to move beyond schools and expanded the portfolio of their services to build the skills of the youth and adults in the community. This move included empowering them with employability skills, digital literacy, financial literacy, and more.

Anjlee knew that technology could help catalyze change in education across India into the 21st century. But at the time, Learning Links Foundation, as a nonprofit, simply lacked the resources to implement technology and innovation projects without the support of donors. This obstacle did not curtail Anjlee's vision and mission. Teams at the nonprofit began outreach to large technology corporations, and slowly, some began to respond. The foundation had piqued interest by demonstrating the change that could be made in student learning outcomes as a result of adopting new learning platforms and tools. In other words, Learning Links Foundation showed a demand for their services—and as a result, the organization was able to secure partnerships with companies like Dell, Amazon, Google, and Adobe to support initiatives in STEAM education. With these key partnerships in place and the inclusion of youth and adults as beneficiaries, the organization's profile began to rise exponentially. Today, it is a strong and growing network of collaborations with partners in 27 countries.

Some might ask, "Can an organization scale on passion alone? Wouldn't standardization and processes take over the passion that once drove the team?" Enter persistence! According to Anjlee, there are two key things that she has kept consistent throughout the years. The first is the value of taking care of the team at all costs. She strongly states that there is never shame in asking for help, which is something that she does often and facilitates by arranging peer-to-peer mentoring networks throughout the organization. She also pays attention to each employee's interests—in her words, "the cause that drives them"—to make sure that their goals are aligned with the organization's and that they are feeling personally fulfilled. If they aren't, Anjlee works with them to redesign their roles or transition into other parts of the organization. She rarely, if ever, gives up on employees, even when there are challenges and failures. "Because of this," Anjlee says, "we have a culture where people take care of each other."

The second value Anjlee has instilled in the organization and kept consistent throughout the years is to continue to give her team the autonomy to execute Learning Links' vision in the way they think best serves the beneficiary. The initial quick growth of the organization meant that each employee needed to be entrepreneurial and think quickly on their feet. There wasn't always going to be a clear pathway, a yes or no answer, or a "right" way to do things—they had to trust in their philosophy of building relationships with the communities they were aiming to serve, not micromanage.

To this day, Anjlee's persistence has confounded other leaders who are surprised by how much she entrusts to her team, but the results are clear: The Learning Link Foundation team believes they are leading a transformative movement, not following a step-by-step rule book. Anjlee entrusted her team with the vision and empowered them to build it out in ways that made sense to the communities they helped. This approach required a culture of learning, unlearning, and relearning, which meant accepting that they might not get it right every time. "When you are committed and you have a deep passion to make something happen," Anjlee said, "you will never give up—you will always keep going."

And keep going she has. Even during the COVID-19 crisis of 2020, Learning Links Foundation pivoted to provide children with more holistic well-being and support. They shipped out more than 55,000 learning kits for homeschooling to different parts of India and began to work with 38,000 children on WhatsApp to facilitate remote learning. "Catastrophes and challenges bring out skills and strengths like never before," she said. "Now, more than ever, women and communities are taking responsibility for children's learning, which was not happening earlier. We want to hold on to that and leverage that for the future. We can't give up; we must work with our stakeholders to continue to engage the whole village in educating a child."

The Learning Links Foundation is an extraordinary organization. The autonomy given to each team member has freed them up to serve communities on an individual level and exercise their own passion to make an impact in the way that works best for the beneficiary. Anjlee's persistence in striving for systemic change has led to her conviction that collaborative models with both government and community participation work best. This persistence is built into the DNA of Learning Links Foundation, and Anjlee's commitment to playing the role of the facilitator of resources has promoted a sense of agility in the company, making room for growth as it continues to impact India in unprecedented ways.-

Lessons Learned from Passion

The women we interviewed said that leaning into their passion, showing interpersonal sensitivity for those they were trying to help, and maintaining persistence in finding new, innovative solutions to ongoing problems were essential to any key role on their team—far more so than one's college education or their GPA. This formula suggests that these entrepreneurial traits and skills are not just important for leading an organization but are crucial in hiring and management strategies. Megan Harney, one of the InnovateHERs interviewed, stated, "I hire only people who are as passionate as I am!" Across the board, that was the most important hiring filter for leaders who scored highly on passion.

When combined with interpersonal sensitivity and persistence, passion can be a powerful driver of change. When given direction with a purpose, it can lead to tangible results and incredibly successful social impact initiatives. However, if a leader has not developed a sense of empathy or persistence, or if they haven't built a team that emulates these skills, they can be overly forceful, volatile, or end up chasing a fantasy. Modeling empathy for others and learning persistence over time is crucial for any leader who has passion as a personality trait.

Importantly: If you feel like you are passionate but haven't found a purpose yet—fear not. They are two separate things. Purpose-driven work can shift and evolve throughout someone's life, but your passionate personality trait will stick with you. While the direction your passion is pointed in may change, your ability to get excited about something, find your work motivating, and express your belief in a cause will help you to attract resources and be effective as an advocate for any cause.

Zoë and Anjlee's stories show how living with passion and approaching your work with excitement and joy can help you sustain the growth of an organization over a long period of time. Passion is a superpower, and our research and interviews reveal two key insights:

1. Passion drives the majority of those who lead purpose-driven organizations.
2. However, interpersonal sensitivity (empathy) and persistence are what help passionate leaders stand out among leaders and have an outsized impact in their field.

Working with passion is crucial in the purpose-driven economy. Whether you are starting your own organization or looking to transition roles into another company or nonprofit, remember that the way you approach your work—with excitement, joy, interpersonal sensitivity, and persistence—is just as important as your other credentials.

To help demonstrate the importance of these attributes, we've included the following sections throughout the next chapters about entrepreneurial mindset personality traits and skills: the InnovateHER Bootcamp.

In the InnovateHER Bootcamp sections, we distill the lessons learned from our research into a step-by-step process that shows how exemplary InnovateHERs applied their unique entrepreneurial traits and learned skills to achieve their goals. By breaking down their stories into small parts, we provide a simple framework to show how an entrepreneurial mindset can be leveraged for success. Additionally, you can use this structure to think about *your* unique entrepreneurial traits and skills and how you can use them to overcome challenges in your career.

InnovateHER Bootcamp:

Using Passion, Empathy, and Persistence to Build a Complex Product

Patricia Scanlon—SoapBox Labs

BACKGROUND

Patricia Scanlon had 16 years of experience working as an engineer and a researcher on the cutting edge of voice AI technology before starting her deep tech company, SoapBox Labs. With a PhD in Speech Recognition and Artificial Intelligence and now nearly 25 years of experience to her name, Patricia is one of the leading experts in Europe when it comes to voice technology.

PROBLEM

Patricia faced two main challenges at the beginning of her career: keeping up with her fast-paced job at Bell Labs and caring for her three-year-old daughter, who enjoyed playing with educational apps. One day, Patricia began to casually observe her daughter using an early literacy app. There was a quiz at the end, and she watched as her daughter randomly guessed the answers until—bing! The right choice. When Patricia asked her daughter what she had just learned, she received a blank stare in return. Her daughter clearly wasn't "learning" anything. The wheels started turning in Patricia's mind, and she thought back to the many papers she had read about artificial intelligence and early literacy. Why wasn't there a speech component to it, where her daughter would have to repeat back to the tablet what she had just heard? She went back to the research and found a trove of insights about how voice technology fails children, and all kinds of population subsets, such as people with diverse accents, poor literacy or language development skills, or for whom English is a foreign language, and many more. Could she develop a technology that would do a better job of capturing those voices to improve literacy?

LEVERAGING PASSION

During her five years as a PhD researcher, the one thing that pushed Patricia forward was passion for her work. She has always been deeply engaged in the work she does and especially enjoys the visionary aspects of the job. She says she's happiest when envisioning the future of technology and attributes to that curiosity and passion her success in fundraising and attracting world-class talent into SoapBox Labs, well before the company had released the product to the market.

APPLYING PERSISTENCE

"My biggest concern was that for too long, too many people had been kicking mediocre speech recognition products into the market, and the resulting voice experience for people was very disappointing. I knew it would take a significant investment in time and resources to build a solution that understood all kids' voices and could transcribe their speech accurately." Getting her PhD had taught her some persistence, but it was nothing like the challenges that lay ahead in entrepreneurship. Accurate Voice AI for kids would take years to research and develop, require millions of euros to fund, and would need a top-notch team of engineers, computational linguists, and scientists to crack a problem that no one else, at that time, had been able to solve. She continued to build upon the foundation of persistence she began building during her PhD. As an entrepreneur, she designed, fundraised, recruited, and finally brought a solution to market that could empower students—and their teachers—on the challenging and empowering journey to literacy fluency.

BUILDING EMPATHY

The biggest challenge in building voice technology that works for all kids has been making sure there are no biases built into the models. Patricia and her team had to develop a deep and empathetic knowledge of their end users—how kids speak, behave, the environments they inhabit, and their privacy needs. Their voice technology had to work with kids of all accents and dialects, which meant covering an incredible range of racial and ethnic groups, educational backgrounds, and socio-economic circumstances. Her ambition was to deliver voice experiences to kids that delighted them, that brought them joy, and that empowered them by accurately recognizing their voices. The SoapBox speech technology has been embedded into third-party products around the globe that support kids in developing and enhancing their literacy and language skills, as well as learning through play in engaging apps and games.

OUTCOME

Patricia has raised over €10.5 million since the launch of SoapBox to research and develop voice AI technology for children ages 2–12. SoapBox now licenses its voice technology to large education, media, games, and toy companies worldwide. She has been recognized as one of the world's visionaries in voice by Voicebot.ai and is listed by Forbes as one of the world's Top 50 Women in Tech. SoapBox is a success, and Patricia's passion for equity in voice AI, persistence in getting the resources to build her product, and personal sensitivity for her end users have resulted in SoapBox's proprietary and award-winning voice technology for kids—the most accurate and private voice solution on the market today.

CHAPTER 4

Need to Achieve + Persistence + Idea Generation + Execution

Imagine that it's *9:59 p.m., and you're the last one in the office. As the lights dim, your colleagues are throwing their laptops into their cases and muttering, "Have a good night," as they quickly walk by to make the last train. You stretch out in your chair and stare up at the ceiling. Why are you always the last one in the office? Is it that you are always raising your hand for new assignments and opportunities? Maybe you just need to be more efficient. Did you really need that*

30-minute coffee break? But that promotion is only a few late nights away...

If this narrative sounds familiar, it's likely that you are an InnovateHER with a strong need to achieve. You aren't alone. *Need to achieve*, "the desire to achieve at a high level,"[2] is engrained in the psyches of many successful women. Our research at the University of Pennsylvania revealed that this perceived need was by far the strongest personality trait in women educational leaders. This makes sense. There are typically only a select few high-ranking positions in leadership, so those who get those positions must be ambitious. Why is the need to achieve not listed in the book as the *most* relevant and important trait? **Because the women we interviewed self-reported *passion* almost three times as much as they self-reported *need to achieve*.**

When we set out to interview the InnovateHERs, we thought it would be safe to assume that since the need to achieve was the most defining trait of a purpose-driven leader in our University of Pennsylvania study, it would come up as an important theme in the interviews...right? However, the exact opposite happened. **The *need to achieve* was without a doubt the most taboo of all the InnovateHER traits and the least mentioned in our interviews.** Some of the women we spoke to even had a negative reaction to being called "ambitious." Instead, they preferred to attribute their success to luck or a great network of support. This explanation was baffling. Clearly, the need to achieve is not as warm and fuzzy as passion or as inspiring as calculated risk-taking. Regardless, how could these women diverge so greatly from the results of the research?

After several interviews, we began to shift our questioning around the need to achieve. We realized that the InnovateHERs lit up when talking about the profound impact their positions allowed them to have. Clearly, whether explicitly or implicitly stated, the need to achieve manifested as the InnovateHERs striving to do more, to do it better, and to significantly impact the people they served. The women we spoke with were not at all ashamed about their desire to grow their organizations and create a positive impact in the world but appeared to avoid describing themselves, alongside this desire, as "ambitious." But this avoidance doesn't change the fact that when the mission is personal, InnovateHERs with a strong need to achieve make unstoppable social impact leaders. As stated by the former Chief of Protocol for Canada, Margaret Huber, "I come from a refugee, working-class background. My family deeply prized education, which is portable. They taught me that you can achieve *and* make an impact—and that success isn't necessarily about money but to contribute and leave something positive behind you."

Wanting to *do well* for yourself and to *do good* for others is an incredibly powerful combination for leaders of purpose-driven organizations and leads to the development of other skills that enable success. Three skills stood out: persistence, idea generation, and execution. We'll explore these skills in the stories of Sabari Raja and Nisha Ligon, and then we'll pose the question, "What does it mean to achieve for oneself *and* to make an impact?"

Sabari Raja's Story: From a Rural Farm to the Corporate Boardroom

Portrait of an InnovateHER: Need to Achieve + Persistence

Even as a ten-year-old girl, Sabari Raja knew that if she did not pursue a college education and a career after finishing high school, she would have to endure the social pressure to get married early. Although she always aspired to have a career, she did not have much exposure to professional women outside of her limited environment. Entrepreneurship was outside of the realm of possibility for her—at least that was the case until she first set eyes on the Biocon campus in Bangalore, India.

Every year, she looked forward with great anticipation to spending her summer holiday with her uncle and aunt in Bangalore—the "Silicon Valley" of India. She loved visiting them because their world was very different and intriguing to her. During her visits, she would accompany her uncle to work. One summer, on the way to his company, he pointed out the sprawling campus of Biocon and asked, "Do you know who started this company?" She shook her head. "Kiran Mazumdar Shah," he responded. Her eyes widened. "The company was started by a *woman*?" she asked, and her uncle laughed and nodded. Coming from a conservative background, she was shocked to find out that a woman was running the largest biotechnology company in India. The idea that a woman could start a company, let alone grow it into a multimillion-dollar business, sparked a fire inside of Sabari.

"When I think back to all the moments in my life, I wonder, when did I really aspire to become an entrepreneur? I think that experience was a game changer," she said. "The minute I heard [Kiran's] story, it became my aspiration. I was always trying to be something big. I want to achieve. I want to get to the next level. But seeing Biocon changed me deeply. To me, owning my own business became my ultimate level of success."

However, the ten-year-old Sabari had a long way to go before reaching that dream. Her story begins on a small coconut farm in Southern India, and her uncle in Bangalore was one of a few relatives who had broken the family tradition of being a farmer. If she were to stay in her village, her destiny would be to marry and continue the family tradition of farming. Her parents also decided to break away from family tradition because they knew they wanted a brighter future for Sabari no matter what the cost was. When she turned five years old, she waved a teary-eyed goodbye to them at the local bus station and set off for boarding school. It was a gut-wrenching decision for her parents to send her so far at such a young age, but like many families, they knew that education was the only path to securing a better and different future for their daughter.

The implicit message to Sabari was clear: Study hard, get good grades, and take advantage of every opportunity presented to you. From five years old onward, she understood her parents' sacrifice—and she also felt the weight of their expectations. Sabari was determined to be the best. She spent late nights studying at her desk and worked long hours to exceed all the normal indicators for success. As a little girl, she dreamed that, as an educated woman, she could become a doctor, lawyer, engineer, or get a corporate job. But that unexpected detour on a summer vacation with her uncle to Bangalore planted an entrepreneurial seed in her and allowed her to dream bigger than anything she ever previously imagined. *What if I could create the jobs others would want?*

Those who know Sabari best listen to her grand plans and dreams with sighs, shakes of the head, and knowing looks. But they also know that when she sets her mind to something, her need to achieve coupled with her persistence makes her formidable when it comes to chasing her dreams and achieving greatness.

After boarding school, Sabari earned a college degree in engineering. As she settled into her adult life, cultural pressure began to mount. She didn't feel ready for marriage and didn't want to get a job in something she wasn't interested in. Her dream of starting a business seemed too distant. She wondered to herself, "Is this it, or is there something else bigger out there?" As she wrestled with her decision and endured some pressure from her extended family, a friend mentioned that she was taking the GRE and planned to pursue higher education in the United States. Without giving it too much thought, Sabari decided she would do the same to buy herself more time. She knew she had to persist just a little bit longer to figure out her next steps.

Within a few months, Sabari was accepted at Louisiana State University. The next thing she knew, she was on a plane for the first time in her life and headed halfway across the world. All was going according to plan until the wheels hit the tarmac on her connecting flight through Germany. Staring out the window, her decision struck her like a ton of bricks—she had never felt further from home. "What was I thinking?" she thought to herself. As she started the second leg of her journey, she began to cry. Everyone looked strange, and even worse, she had no idea what any of the food options were on the in-flight menu. "I'm going to buy a plane ticket back the second I land. This whole plan is insane."

She felt she had already made the decision to turn back, but once the initial shock wore off, she began to reason with herself. She had already come so far. She had worked so hard for this. By the time she landed in the US, the little voice in the back of her head had begun to whisper a different tune. "I have already made it this far, and I have so much to accomplish. It's not time to go home yet. I still need to get to the next step." She took a deep breath and decided to double down on her original plan. She got off the plane and began her new life in the United States.

The next chapter of Sabari's story follows a similar arc to many who have immigrated to the US to pursue a new career: She graduated from school and got her first job as a software engineer, working her way up the corporate ladder from there. Though she struggled with self-confidence and finding her voice, she found important mentors and allies along the way who pushed her to step out of her comfort zone. All was going well until she volunteered to take a new position as the Emerging Market Development Expert and was sent back to India for eight months. Now married and with two small children, she welcomed this new opportunity even though she knew the risks involved. "I needed that job to get to the next level. So, of course I'm going to go for it, right? Those are the opportunities that strengthened my leadership profile," she said.

But when she returned to India, even at the pinnacle of her career and more successful than ever, self-doubt began to bubble up. She began wondering, "Where am I going to go after this? What am I really trying to accomplish? What is my end goal?" She realized that, in the pursuit of corporate success, she had forgotten her original dream to become an entrepreneur.

This is a pivotal moment in the career of many entrepreneurs. She knew what she wanted to do—and that was to quit, to start something of her own. On top of that, just like her trip to the United States, she knew that if she didn't do it now, she never would. The decision was only complicated by her strong need to achieve. How would she measure success without the traditional framework of being promoted, earning responsibilities, and getting raises? She sat down, had a serious conversation with her husband, and decided that she was going to give herself two years to get something off the ground. She trusted the same persistence that brought her success to date while also recognizing something she conveyed to us during our interview: "Innovation doesn't happen from having a rigid structure. I feel like most of my creative thinking and innovation happens when I'm not so strict in my processes and structures." So, she kept going and stuck to her plan. One failed business attempt and exactly two years later, Nepris was born.

Nepris is a platform that connects learners and educators to real-world industry experts. With over 165,800 educators enrolled, more than 50 employees, and a growing list of 55,000 industry professionals from hundreds of companies, it's on track to become a formidable force in the EdTech space. Much like Sabari's experience seeing Biocon as a little girl, she recognized the importance of connecting students to real-world experts so they could witness for themselves the opportunities that exist outside of the four walls of their home or the classroom. Nepris is at the intersection of personal purpose and social impact, creating the perfect conditions for an impactful, purpose-driven organization. Sabari, leading with a need to achieve, followed by her persistence to live the kind of life she envisioned, shows how the combination of these entrepreneurial traits and skills can drive women to do big things.

Need to Achieve and Persistence

If you were nodding at different parts of Sabari's story, you too may have a very close relationship with the need to achieve. It might be a healthy relationship, or it might be a harmful one—but the odds are that this drive has a definitive presence in your career choices. Many studies have investigated the root causes of *why* women have a strong need to achieve, but for our purposes, the most important factor is to understand *how* it influences InnovateHERs' careers. In our conversations with the InnovateHERs, our goal was to discover how their desire to achieve at high levels manifested, and we observed it in three different ways.

The first way that the InnovateHERs' need to achieve appeared was in discussion of the impact their organizations have had. They were proud of the social change their organization was generating and were eager to show what their businesses or nonprofits had accomplished during their leadership tenure. This, to us, spoke to a desire to produce excellent quality and respected work. The second way this entrepreneurial personality trait appeared was through expressing high expectations for their own and their teams' performances. Though they proudly shared their teams' accomplishments, in some cases they minimized their own or attributed their success to their desire to make a change instead of their traits and skills. We interpreted this tendency to mean that even though InnovateHERs were hesitant to take credit for their own accomplishments, they were very proud of the accomplishments that their teams and organizations had made, signaling that they placed value on high achievement. Lastly, they discussed the fear of failure and the desire to live up to their stakeholders' expectations—this was especially due to the few leadership positions and opportunities women receive. But most of all, they felt pressured to perform well for the people their organizations were built to serve.

If you are an InnovateHER who scores high on the need to achieve, you might read Eckerd College's definition, "the desire to achieve at a high level"[2] and feel a familiar knot of despair in your gut similar to what you might have felt reading the scenario at the beginning of the chapter. The vagueness of this definition for an overachiever raises questions like, "What exactly is a *high level?* Where is the bar for achievement, and...am I there yet?"

Untangling achievements for personal gain from achievements for the greater good is thorny, which is why it is so crucial to tell tangible and real stories of how this trait plays a role in driving success for InnovateHERs. On a personal level, a list of achievements such as awards received, prestigious university titles, or major milestones checked off can signal the need to achieve but doesn't necessarily provide the full picture. You can want the world, but you must build persistence over time before success can manifest itself. Getting comfortable talking about how the need to achieve influences your life in both positive and negative ways on the path to success is deeply important in having honest conversations about success.

As reflected in Sabari's story, persistence drives the need to achieve. It's that little voice in your head that asks, "What's next?" or "Is this the best you can do?" It often is a little pushy, hard to quiet down, and is what wakes you up in the middle of the night as you get close to an upcoming deadline—you're not there, *yet.* Need to achieve shows up years before the awards, promotions, and milestones do, so persistence must accompany it the whole way through. It can drive you to take risks or jump into action when feeling uncertain and help you overcome massive barriers, as Sabari did.

It is important to note that when this trait is not channeled productively, it can show up in several harmful ways, such as perfectionism, blind ambition, or becoming a workaholic. Though some of those traits coincide with factors important for building big teams (like work ethic), others (like perfectionism) can be counterproductive. When the need to achieve shows up as one of your strongest attributes, launching your own business might not be the right path for you. You may benefit more from the structured milestones that a traditional job offers, and there is nothing wrong with that. However, because of how predominant the need to achieve is, we have deemed this entrepreneurial personality trait the keystone in the Portrait of an InnovateHER. Quietly, but essential to holding an organization together, the need to achieve is a central quality that purpose-driven leaders frequently embody.

Effective InnovateHERs have another skill combination that matches nicely with need to achieve: the ability to dream big using idea generation and executing to make those dreams reality. This is a skill combination allows for the adaptability and agility commonly found in high-performing organizations. Combine it with persistence, and a leader can sustain progress over time and manifest a truly transformative organization.

Nisha Ligon's Story: Dreaming Big and Acting Now to Make an Impact

Portrait of an InnovateHER: Need to Achieve +
Idea Generation + Execution

Each morning of March 2020, Nisha Ligon woke up and religiously refreshed the news from her bedroom. She was watching incredulously as the COVID-19 crisis unfolded around the world. The implications for the lockdowns that elected officials were suggesting were enormous. Could it be possible that 240 million students would be out of school for an undefined time? What would this absence mean for students across rural areas of the African continent—where her nonprofit, Ubongo, is based? These students counted on school as a community center and hub for learning. How would those students who didn't have access to the internet at home learn? As the CEO of an educational content creation organization, she knew her team needed to move fast. Nisha's ability to realize her dreams helped Ubongo reach millions of children and build a bridge to allow students to continue learning, despite the most challenging environment for education we have seen in over 100 years.

Before we dive into the story of how Ubongo adapted to the times in 2020, Nisha shares that entrepreneurship was not always a fixed path for her. Unlike Sabari, she did not have entrepreneurial aspirations from a young age. True, she was born to entrepreneurial parents, but she fully planned on having a traditional pathway. She went to a competitive magnet school, which led her to become a biology major at an Ivy League university, where she completed a study abroad program in Tanzania and was perfectly content to proceed to film school, where she hoped to become a documentary filmmaker. She has always been an overachiever—as her resume attests—and she liked the idea of a straightforward career path. But it wasn't until she met Laura Poitras, a successful documentarian who taught a documentary film workshop at Yale, that she even began to consider alternative pathways that sparked her entrepreneurial spirit.

During a six-month exchange program in Tanzania in college, Nisha had made a few short films. Hesitant to get feedback, she apprehensively mentioned them to her professor after class and asked for advice on where to apply for graduate school. "What if," Poitras asked her, "you were to go out and spend all that money you were going to spend on grad school on making a movie? You already know how to do it." Something clicked inside of her. Nisha is the type of person who makes things happen. Maybe it was living on a farm where there was always work to do and problems to solve, or maybe it was her entrepreneurial parents who pushed her to take on responsibility for her own life starting at a young age, but she likes to get her hands dirty and do the work. The advice Poitras gave her simply made sense and aligned with her instincts and values. So, she decided to forego graduate school and become a documentary filmmaker sooner than she expected, aiming to make her dream a reality. In fact, she already had the subject matter for her documentary: women's football in Tanzania.

She mapped out the idea of the film, secured fiscal sponsorship, and within a few months, she was filming. But after filming wrapped and she began preparing for film festivals, she began to get a sinking feeling in her stomach that the film wouldn't have the impact she desired. Though important issues like gender equity and education were covered, there weren't any action items for viewers to pursue after seeing the film. Intuitively, she knew that showing a video about Tanzania in the western world would have little to no impact on a community that she had grown to care about so deeply. She confirmed that feeling after screenings of film festivals back home in the US. If this film wouldn't provide that kind of impact, what would?

No matter which way she turned, she came back to education. "Education is such an amazing tool. I see it as a lever for fixing so many other problems that we have in the world," she said. "I'm one of those people who kind of cares about every issue. And at the end of the day, when you give the next generation a good foundational education, then you're really setting up the next generation of changemakers. It touches absolutely everything." Her next step was brainstorming what kind of impact she wanted to have on education, given her skill sets—filmmaking, idea execution, and envisioning systemic solutions to problems. She knew her inner need to achieve would help her accomplish her mission. She just needed to find the right team.

Ubongo was formed with the broad mission of improving education in Africa. Someone else with the propensity for idea generation might have gotten lost in the grandiosity of the vision. But the combination of idea generation and execution, as well as her need to achieve, helped Nisha set things into motion quickly. With four other co-founders, they spread out across different regions of the continent and began market research. They found that students were disengaged in school and began brainstorming ideas for how to solve that problem. They decided that if they could combine best practices from what they knew about engaging filmmaking and content creation and couple that with Nisha's background in educational media, they could create engaging, animated content for kids in school. They decided to start with math: Break down complex concepts into simple, easy-to-understand videos that would be provided for free. If that went well, they would expand into other educational areas.

After a few pivots from for-profit to nonprofit and testing the value proposition at pitch competitions and with users, they finally decided on a nonprofit model. They grew the team to 49 people and began seeing growth in their content views not only in Sub-Saharan and Eastern Africa but also in the US and internationally. When COVID-19 hit, they began to see demand grow by the thousands. The decision to become a nonprofit had never been more relevant. They shifted their target to ensure more children had free access to their content. Their target user—a family with a child who could access TV or radio but not the internet—grew exponentially. They released all of their TV and radio content under free licenses so that broadcasters, governments, educators, and parents could use and share them to keep children learning. With schools closing, they suddenly became the main source of educational content for millions of students in 18 countries across Africa. Ubongo had found its niche.

With this explosion of growth, Nisha had satisfied her need to achieve, as she was positively impacting millions of children across Africa. However, she began to realize that her love for executing ideas and working creatively was holding her team back as the organization's growth exploded. She also recognized that the skillset of growing a successful multi-country organization was very different from that which she'd drawn upon to build and launch a product and startup. Lastly, she recognized the importance of an African leading an organization that made edutainment in Africa, for Africa. Nisha shared with her board and team that she'd like to find a growth-stage CEO for Ubongo, one who could help the growing organization flourish through its next stage of the company's growth. As a new leader joins Ubongo, Nisha will transition out of the CEO position and into a creative and innovation-focused role where she can continue to draw upon her strengths to achieve Ubongo's mission while also supporting a new leader who will bring her own skillset to grow and lead the organization.

Nisha exemplifies how a unique skillset—the ability to think big with idea generation and execute quickly and efficiently—combined with a deep-rooted need to achieve led her to follow her instincts and leverage her networks to create an effective purpose-driven organization. Her personality is encoded into her organization. The quick pivot during COVID-19, the ability to attract resources, and the aim to reach as many students as possible in a way that allowed them to stay connected positioned Ubongo to rise to meet the moment and have a widespread, positive impact during a time of crisis.

Lessons Learned from Need to Achieve

Need to achieve was hands-down the hardest entrepreneurial trait to understand in our conversations. So many of the InnovateHERs didn't consider themselves high achievers, and until it was placed in the context of helping or leading their organization to achieve its purpose, they were hesitant to discuss wanting to achieve for themselves. But when we asked about how they handled the pressure of running a purpose-driven organization, about using key metrics to show results in their organizations, and the connection between their passion and their work, their eyes lit up, and the trait was immediately identifiable.

The InnovateHERs rarely addressed this personality trait directly; in fact, we heard very little about prizes, awards, or academic achievements. Instead, the role of ambition in their career was coded into the answers they gave. It became clear to us that need to achieve is an uncomfortable topic of conversation when it comes to thinking about societal stereotypes of women, who are often taught to hide ambition to seem likable or more collaborative. Ambition is often wrongly given a negative connotation, insinuating self-absorption or a win-at-all-costs attitude. On some occasions, the InnovateHERs we interviewed rejected the notion that a drive to *do well for themselves* was a motivator of their success. Instead, they preferred to attribute their success to their desire to *do good for others*. While that may be true, we were interested in understanding how it drove them to the top of their organizations and sectors. The follow-up question then became, "But what does your personal ambition have to do with your success? What was in this for *you*, and what did you hope to gain from your achievements?"

Placing the trait in context clarified that need to achieve does not work in isolation. We found that if you have it in your personality, chances are it extends beyond the workplace. Think about your childhood—were you ever called an overachiever? Many of the women we interviewed had been given that label. We saw time and again that the need to be excellent crossed into their personal lives. They often referenced the importance of keeping their families as their top priority and how they struggled to "make it all work." Stories of gut-wrenching decisions to move to a new country, go back to school, bootstrap an organization while working a full-time job, or quit a job with cushy benefits to begin a startup all meant personal sacrifices that were difficult for many to reconcile. Especially for those who had decided to become mothers, the so-called "mom guilt" was consistently present as they pursued their career goals. The question was omnipresent: Is it possible to achieve at all levels? And does the need to achieve ever hinder progress?

These challenges track with a well-known study that came out of the Harvard Business School in 2014, which proved that while women and men were now both striving to achieve success in a holistic way that included family and career, high-achieving women were up to 20 percent less satisfied than men were with the reality of working and raising a family.[23] This tension was also echoed by many women who had started their own businesses. While many cited the importance or influence of their families in their lives, they struggled to do it all well and referenced feelings of frustration over their efforts never being enough. Specifically, with the women who self-identified as high achievers, it was clear that doing anything less than the best was considered a failure.

Need to achieve, persistence, idea generation, and execution are all essential skills to help InnovateHERs achieve key metrics. However, when the need to achieve trait becomes overwhelming, there is another external element that serves as a great counterbalance: *mentorship.* For those who demonstrated a tendency to overachieve *and* hold themselves to unrealistic standards of excellence, it was almost essential to have an external network of support including mentors to provide support and guidance. Further explored throughout the stories and in Chapter 9, we share the critical role that women mentors play in helping high-achieving women navigate decisions that involve tough trade-offs. The women we interviewed explained how having a community of experienced, empathic professional women helped them to manage their need to achieve. They modeled and shared how to address missteps and mistakes and then, most importantly, how to practice a little self-forgiveness and grace.

Need to achieve is clearly a key driver of an InnovateHER's success. It is perhaps the most unrelenting, insistent trait out of them all—but at the same time, it is one of the most crucial in having an impact on a large scale. From our interviews, we learned the following:

1. A leader who has a healthy need to achieve drives growth in organizations.
2. When broken down into achievable goals and combined with persistence, idea generation, and execution, need to achieve can be an incredibly powerful catalyst for growth.

Sabari and Nisha's stories show us how, when focused, the need to achieve can drive your purpose forward, push you through fears, and help you make an impact. It can be the motivator behind building entrepreneurial skills—like persistence, idea generation, and execution—that ultimately lead you to become successful in your career and to have a positive impact on a bigger audience than you had ever imagined.

InnovateHER Bootcamp:

Using Need to Achieve, Idea Generation/Execution, and Persistence

Margaret Huber, Former Ambassador and Chief of Protocol of Canada

BACKGROUND

Margaret Huber grew up in Canada in a family of immigrants who came from war-torn Europe. Her family deeply valued education and achievement as social mobility tools, encouraging her to shine at school from a young age. Margaret understood how important it was to excel throughout her academic career. Later, as a diplomat, Margaret undertook postings in three different continents throughout her career in the Canadian Foreign Service. She has served in multiple countries and now reflects on how she used her own drive to achieve with teams of high-achieving and purposeful diplomats.

PROBLEM

Diplomats must be adaptable. Each time they move countries, they need to reinvent themselves. They need to respect and understand differences and adapt to foreign cultures and customs. They have a clear mission for their country but also need to understand and react in real time to challenges with little guidance. It is an entrepreneurial job within government that requires a commitment to excellence and grit and the ability to understand the big picture while also executing independently on the vision. Margaret built those skills throughout her 40-year career in the service, but as the Chief of Protocol, she had a new assignment: connecting with her team to do the same thing. Could these skills be taught, she wondered, or were they innate?

LEVERAGING NEED TO ACHIEVE

Margaret knew from personal experience that successful diplomats need to be self-motivated. It's not easy to arrive in a new country and adapt to the local customs. Additionally, diplomats have the challenge of representing their government—but often their bosses are on the other side of the world. The job requires someone who is internally motivated to do well and inherently cares about the work. According to Margaret, you need to hire for that skill; it is essential for someone who will have to operate independently while still representing the interests of their home country.

APPLYING IDEA GENERATION AND EXECUTION ABILITIES

Foreign service members must understand the mission. This part can be learned through a collaborative process of understanding the challenges the country faces, how you can support them, and what role your government can play. By the time diplomats are on-site in their assigned country, they need to be ready to act. As the Chief of Protocol, it was Margaret's job not only to create clear guidance on values and processes but also to foster an environment allowing those in the field the space to act independently. The skill of idea generation (thinking big) and then executing (getting the job done) is a unique combination that must be included in all diplomatic training programs. "You won't always get detailed instructions!" Margaret says to her trainees. "You need to know how to make a judgment call. When the stakes are high and you need to act, it is better to ask for forgiveness than for permission."

BUILDING PERSISTENCE

Developing staff in the foreign service requires enormous persistence that can be established over the trajectory of a career.

This skill, according to Margaret, can and should be shared with the next generation. Margaret compares mentoring to gardening, especially planting seeds, which over time may wonderfully flourish. She has watched young staff colleagues overcome challenges, fight through and learn from mistakes, and at the end of the day, reap the rewards. Margaret also warns that the young women coming up in the service will need to develop twice the persistence. There may be less opportunity to speak their minds, especially in more conservative countries. Creating support networks of other women in the Foreign Service can empower and encourage while also reinforcing persistence and tenacity.

OUTCOME

At the end of the day, Margaret was successful in her mission and helped to build the next generation of diplomats in Canada. She credits the opportunity to share skills and values to the positive culture of the Foreign Service. Even though she is now retired, she continues to actively promote programs to mentor young talent interested in international affairs. In addition, she devotes time to various boards and advises nonprofit organizations working to advance democracy and global health.

CHAPTER 5

Calculated Risk + Optimism + Empathy

Think about a risk-taker. Who comes to mind?

Is it someone who jumps out of an airplane to skydive? Is it an investor who puts all their eggs in one basket, betting on the success of one company? Or maybe it's an athlete putting their career on the line to make a bold political statement? Perhaps, like many people, you think of a high-growth entrepreneur. Risk-taking is so synonymous with entrepreneurship that it would be impossible to write a book about entrepreneurial mindset without mentioning it. The stereotype of a risk-taker in the startup world is predominantly that of a young, male entrepreneur with nothing to lose. But knowing some of the women we do, and listening to their stories, this perception of risk-taking as a precursor for entrepreneurial success didn't fit with the narratives we were hearing.

In fact, the more we discussed risk, both of us—Kathy and Bobbi—agreed that some of the riskiest moves we saw were being made by women who were picking up and moving their families across the world for a new opportunity or quitting their corporate jobs in their highest earning potential years to pursue a dream project. They were taking more than just financial risks—they were risking their personal identities. Risks were even greater for women who came from underrepresented communities, as they felt they had less space to fail. Upon embarking on this book, one of our initial driving questions was, "What does risk-taking look like for women, and how does it differ from the traditionally male stereotype?"

We learned two key things from looking at our data through the lens of the Entrepreneurial Mindset Profile®:

1. Entrepreneurial people are bigger risk-takers than are non-entrepreneurs.
2. Entrepreneurial women still have a lower acceptance of risk than men do.

This confirmed part of our assumption. The EMP data shows that entrepreneurs rank higher on the risk spectrum than corporate managers do. Intuitively, it makes sense that traditional entrepreneurs take more risks than the average person. Forging a new path, like starting a business or creating a new program within another organization, implies a large degree of uncertainty, which in turn implies exposure to risk. This image also tracks with the stereotype of an entrepreneur that we previously had.

Interestingly, this trend breaks down when we regard those working for or starting purpose-oriented organizations. The educational leaders surveyed in our research at the University of Pennsylvania scored approximately 8 percentage points higher on risk acceptance than did corporate managers, but 4 percentage points below those starting businesses and new initiatives in other non-purpose-driven sectors, like food and beverage or construction.[5] Hence, purpose-driven entrepreneurs are naturally more risk-averse and less likely to gamble than are traditional entrepreneurs.

Interestingly, a closer look at the EMP data also revealed that men are more likely to be risk-takers than women, and entrepreneurial men ranked the highest on the risk-taking spectrum. But why would men be more likely to take risks than women?

We set out to further explore this point in our interviews with the InnovateHERs. We heard the women describe themselves as "risk mitigators" and "risk managers" rather than "risk-takers" and "risk seekers."[24] Their self-described processes for starting new projects and ventures often involved performing research, forming personal connections with their potential end users, and holding a no-failure policy for their ideas, especially when it came to products in the school space as well as in the corporate learning space. Many cited their drive to work their way out of failure. The risk of failing their users, beneficiaries, or customers—especially when vulnerable populations were involved—was simply unacceptable.

The market is responding to purpose-driven people's tension between their desire to do good and their unwillingness to fail the people they serve by creating resources to help mitigate risk. Organizations like the EDUCATE Venture Research Lab in London are providing research teams for entrepreneurs developing EdTech products so that more people can utilize high-quality research to create products that align with the best practices in pedagogy and learning design. Other organizations, as with the Education Research and Development Institute (ERDI), are connecting entrepreneurs directly to networks of educational leaders so that they can get feedback from customers in real time. Resources such as these and many others help purpose-driven leaders take calculated risks.

Two important characteristics make the risk profile of an InnovateHER unique: lots of optimism and high levels of interpersonal sensitivity (or empathy). These learned skills are important to understand how to mitigate risk so that a fear of failure does not hinder the bold vision that strong, purpose-driven leadership requires.

Sherrie Westin's Story: An Unexpected Purpose

Portrait of an InnovateHER: Risk + Optimism

"You can't take a risk if you don't feel secure," Sherrie Westin said confidently in her interview with us, "because to calculate any risk, you need to take emotion out of the equation, which is almost impossible to do if you don't feel safe. If the risk doesn't work out like you planned, at least you have a solid base that allows you to recover from setbacks."

Sherrie was referring to her own career when she said this, but her words reveal a truth we heard throughout many of our interviews: Purpose-driven women seek to feel secure before taking a risk, and as Sherrie's story demonstrates, InnovateHERs are often inspired to take the leap of faith when the rewards lead to a higher purpose. Sherrie exemplified this quality throughout her career. Calculated risk-taking was a guiding force as she navigated the waters of building toward her current position as the President of Sesame Workshop. Never taking her eyes off the purpose or the "why" behind her risks—to create a better, more equitable world—she has built a positive, long-lasting legacy while making groundbreaking strides in what is possible in the worlds of nonprofits, government, and media.

Sherrie started off as a young professional searching for a way to make a positive impact in the world. Always a calculated risk-taker, she wasn't afraid to speak her mind or boldly explore different areas of interest as she navigated news, communication, and politics. She quickly earned a reputation as someone who was enthusiastic, optimistic, and solution-oriented. She earned the respect of her colleagues in the workplace and began to rise through the ranks. After holding positions in the first Bush Administration—including the highest rank in the White House as Assistant to the President for Public Liaison and Intergovernmental Affairs—she returned to the private sector and the world of media, holding positions at U.S. News & World Report and, a few years later, at ABC Television Network as the Executive Vice President of Network Communications.

At ABC, Sherrie found a fast-paced environment and a level of responsibility that positioned her to influence the status quo. She effectively connected with others, using her optimism to positively influence her colleagues. She honed her ability to delegate—and to feel comfortable with not mastering or being in control of everything—and learned to trust her team to get the job done. She was transforming into the leader she always wanted to be. But still, there was something missing.

Sherrie had previously spent time at ABC News prior to her time at the White House, and she loved being back at ABC in a new role that included overseeing the network's children's programming. After several years in that role, Sherrie adopted her daughter from China at five months of age. As much as she loved her work at ABC, being a new mom hugely increased her focus and interest in the importance of quality children's media. A path to a career pivot was becoming clear. When Joan Ganz Cooney, the creator of *Sesame Street*, approached her to ask if she would ever be interested in joining the Children's Television Workshop (now Sesame Workshop), she felt it was the perfect way to combine her professional interests with that of being a new mom.

"I was so interested in focusing on education and being a new mother," Sherrie reflected during our interview. "I loved that everything I cared most about was finally connected." Her passion for innovation and her tolerance for risk to take newer and bolder chances with the Sesame brand grew as she became more vested in building a better world. With her purpose and passion connected, her career began to skyrocket.

If you grew up watching *Sesame Street*, it shouldn't surprise you that the woman who is now at the helm is a committed optimist who believes it is possible to achieve the best in humanity. What may surprise you is how much she pushed the envelope to expand and grow *Sesame Street*. In 2016, her leadership led to a partnership with the International Rescue Committee, which crossed sectors and borders to support early childhood interventions for children displaced by conflict in the Syrian response region. And in 2017, her ability to think outside the box and reach for new possibilities earned the partnership a coveted $100 million grant from the MacArthur Foundation. She said, "What we're doing is so hard, but if it were easy, it wouldn't be worth doing or somebody else would be doing it. Less than 3 percent of all humanitarian aid goes to education and a tiny sliver of that to early education. On top of that, we have more children displaced than any other time since World War II. How can this be?"

In 2020, Sherrie stepped into the role of President of Sesame Workshop. Since doing so, the nonprofit has produced deeply relevant content about the COVID-19 pandemic and other pressing issues around the world and has also advocated for more inclusive images of families. Sherrie's willingness to take risks driven by her purpose and her optimistic approach has paid off. During her time at Sesame Workshop, she has been named a "Leading Global Thinker" by *Foreign Policy* magazine and one of *Fast Company's* "100 Most Creative People in Business." She was awarded an honorary doctorate degree by Concordia University, and most importantly, her willingness to do what it takes to do what's right has positively impacted the lives of the countless children who watch *Sesame Street* around the world each day.

Sherrie's journey demonstrates that entrepreneurial leaders can take risks when guided by purpose. If you build the skills over time to feel comfortable, you can lean into your optimism and shine a light on a path toward a brighter future. In Sherrie's case, it was making jumps in her career and pioneering new initiatives to make a better world for children.

Sherrie is not alone in her endeavors. The women we interviewed consistently cited that their drive to grow their organizations and reach for new challenges was motivated by a mission greater than themselves. Whether by expanding access to education in India, growing a network of schools in Latin America, or leading cross-sector initiatives to bring record funding to the world's neediest communities, risks that led to growth were always coupled with a deep-seated drive to help others. So, why does risk-taking look different in purpose-driven spaces such as learning and teaching? First, we must scrutinize what risk *is*.

Risk Acceptance and Optimism

The *Cambridge Dictionary* defines risk as "the possibility of something bad happening."[25]

"Something bad" encompasses everything from an ordinary setback, such as a stubbed toe or a simple miscommunication, to an unimaginable life-altering occurrence, like the death of a loved one. This ambiguity is deeply uncomfortable when applied to a purpose-driven organization. We can't tolerate the idea of something bad happening to the very people we are trying to serve—especially because that would imply failing the very people who put their trust in us to guide them.

Here, we have a dilemma. If we accept the premise that people who lead purpose-driven organizations tend to be more cautious, then how can we mitigate risk so that leaders can take the chances necessary for greater rewards? Leaders in the purpose-driven space cannot afford to play it safe, and at the same time, they cannot afford to fail the people they serve or the teams that they lead. This conundrum traps many risk-averse leaders because innovating and breaking with societal norms is a process that inherently involves a certain degree of exposure—and, occasionally, failure. For the InnovateHERs we spoke to, the term *calculated risk* quickly began to permeate our conversations.

As defined by the EMP, *risk* is "a willingness to pursue an idea or a desired goal even when the probability of succeeding is low."[2] This definition is a breath of fresh air simply because it contains an important distinction: *probability*. This distinction makes room for optimism to guide a calculated risk-taking strategy. Instead of focusing on something bad happening, this definition opens *the opportunity for something good to happen*, even if the odds of success are low. This allows for a new and far more positive question to emerge: *What can we achieve if we get this right?*

As Sherrie's story shows us, calculated risk-taking, when combined with optimism, means that we are moving toward a better future. And that, for a purpose-driven InnovateHER, is the most important value. Calculated risks then become worth the chance of failure because there is a better world on the other side of the risk.

Vicky Colbert's Story: Human-Centered Approach to School Design

Portrait of an InnovateHER: Risk + Empathy

"Let's start off with a basic premise," Vicky said during our interview with her, clearing her throat. "If you don't have quality or basic education, nothing can be achieved in society."

When Vicky Colbert set out to investigate what was happening in schools across rural Colombia more than 30 years ago, she was convinced that the future of her country relied on access to quality, basic education for all. At the time, Colombia was in the midst of internal warfare with armed groups and emerging drug lords. The challenge was to support the universalization of primary education—a goal for the entire Latin American region—and improve the quality of basic education for Colombia's most vulnerable children, especially the ones who attended remote, rural, and sometimes invisible multi-grade schools. Fresh out of university, Vicky was chosen to lead a new position within Colombia's Ministry of Education as the National Education Coordinator for Multigrade Schools in Rural Areas. First and foremost, she decided that to be successful, she must investigate firsthand the challenges faced by these multigrade schools, where only one teacher was tasked with educating and managing students of various ages and needs.

She knew right away that the answer wasn't going to come to her in an ivory tower. Vicky was born a risk-taker—and while there were great risks associated with traveling in war-torn territories, her empathy for Colombia's children and her optimism for the future of education drove her into the field to investigate. She had never been one to wait for someone else to fix something for her. Why start now?

Her first investigative journey took her deep into the Andean mountains, where she visited the UNESCO Unitary School Project. There, she met an exceptional teacher named Oscar, a local school-teacher and a charismatic leader in the Unitary School UNESCO Project. He received technical support from UNESCO to initiate a demonstration school to train teachers. She also joined forces with Beryl Levinger, a former Peace Corp Volunteer, who became an education official for USAID. Together, they formed a strong alliance that designed the system that eventually became Escuela Nueva.

This small team of dreamers built on the concept of *escuela unitaria* by introducing strategies that were more technically, politically, and financially viable. Above all else, they had to be easily replicable.

Escuela Nueva was proposing a shift in the learning paradigm from a teacher-centric model to a child-centered one. As such, the school would be more participatory and personalized by applying an active learning approach to help students become self-directed, while teachers were facilitators and not transmitters of knowledge. The new approach introduced a dramatic cultural change, and the team knew they would disrupt the entire belief system of conventional education systems, which dominated both developed and developing countries at the time.

Discussing the launch of Escuela Nueva in our interview, Vicky recalled, "We had to start everything from scratch. I had to look for the money so we could implement the model, find the partnerships, and build the relationships—everything." But the seed for an idea of a student-centric, community-built, and easily replicable model had been planted, and she was ready to fight for it, even at the cost of her job.

When Vicky returned to Bogotá, she had a mission: Get buy-in from government partners to fund a pilot program. It was a risky proposition, given the bureaucracy, but she knew she had to try. Fearlessly, she sat down with bureaucrats to make the case for flipping the teacher-centric classroom model on its head. Unsurprisingly, the reaction was lukewarm. Vicky's optimism and heart for what she was doing was clear, but the entrenchment of the existing model was powerful. For at least a hundred years, Colombia was like the rest of the conventional teacher-centered systems in the world, utilizing the same model—could something this radical really work?

Instead of arguing, Vicky leaned on her instinct, focusing her energy on building a case using empirical evidence from pre-existing schools to orient policy making, and she offered officials several simple, manageable actions to begin implementing. Most importantly, she fought for and recruited rural teachers to join her team in the Ministry of Education. Intuitively, Vicky understood that getting the pilot off the ground required that teachers would be the agents of change. Their communities, their children—their *reality*—needed a voice.

At first, her colleagues mocked the idea. These teachers "didn't even have formal diplomas," according to the bureaucrats. What did they really know? Turns out, they knew a great deal, and their experiences were compelling. With insiders and allies who empathized with the problem on board, the next part of her plan began to gain momentum. After demonstrating that her idea would work in rural contexts, the Ministry agreed to support three pilot programs. These pilots prioritized the interests of the children, with the goal of building their skills rather than focusing on content memorization. As the *real* experts in the field, Vicky tapped the teachers themselves to lead the coalition of programs. The three pilots succeeded, and with that, Escuela Nueva was off to a promising start.

There is much to learn from this self-described "Cinderella story." It started with the most remote, isolated, and vulnerable schools and ended with a world-renowned educational model on how to develop schools of the future—especially in remote, impoverished, and underserved areas. Vicky's model became so successful that it was selected by the World Bank in 1989 as one of the three experiences worldwide that had successfully impacted national policy.

While she worked through the Ministry of Education to secure the universalization of primary education and took risks to do what was right, she understood the shifting winds of politics and administrative changes. To ensure the stabilization of universalized primary education and the quality in the implementation of Escuela Nueva, Vicky founded the Fundación Escuela Nueva (FEN), a Colombian NGO, with the mission to sustain the innovation, preserving its quality and integrity, continuously making improvements and disseminating it worldwide. The Escuela Nueva school model has inspired educational reforms internationally—working mainly through governments—including nations in Latin America, the Caribbean, Asia, and Africa.

Its adaptation to new contexts and populations, such as the Escuela Nueva Learning Circles for migrant and displaced children (Círculos de Aprendizaje) and the urban version of Escuela Nueva (Escuela Activa Urbana), have demonstrated significant results, evidenced in multiple evaluations. These pioneering methods, developed by Vicky and the Fundación Escuela Nueva, led the Ashoka, Skoll, and Schwab Foundation to recognize her as a leading social entrepreneur. She has also received the Citizenship Award from the Clinton Global Initiative and the Henry R. Kravis Prize in Leadership from Claremont McKenna College. In the arena of education, she has received the WISE Prize from the Qatar Foundation and the Inaugural Yidan Prize for Educational Development (among other international recognitions).

Lessons Learned from Risk Acceptance

To listen to Vicky speak is to get a masterclass in leading with the heart while staying humble, curious, and focused. She embodies what makes InnovateHERs stand out—taking calculated risks, putting the interests of the people you serve first, and building a talented team to advance a mission.

Vicky's achievements were not based on traditional strategic leadership frameworks. At the beginning, there were no models, financial projections, or even a competitive analysis. What she used was plain and simple: her gut instinct. Incorporating interpersonal sensitivity, or empathy, as part of her strategy was instinctive; she knew that putting the people who had firsthand experience with the problem at the center of the solution would be crucial to its success. Then, she took risks—both personal and with the Escuela Nueva approach—that were guided by her greater purpose. Finally, she was vindicated by the evidence. Not only was Vicky able to get more buy-in from hard-to-impress stakeholders, but she also distributed ownership so that each person would have a stake in the outcome. By massively flipping the learning paradigm from teacher-focused to student-centric, Vicky's model reformed the teacher's role and increased student literacy. Escuela Nueva has since been implemented in more than 20,000 rural schools across Colombia, and thousands of teachers have been trained in this innovative and sustainable model of education. It has inspired educational reforms worldwide, reaching over 7 million children. This is an impressive impact. At present, through an alliance with the Ministry of Education, FEN is reaching thousands of rural teachers from remote areas of Colombia with its community of practice, Renueva, a virtual campus.

Notably, risk-taking was discussed in two ways in the interviews with InnovateHERs: taking a risk on a *personal level* and taking a risk on an *organizational level.* The women interviewed repeatedly spoke about the necessity of taking risks to achieve their personal missions, but they did so with caution. They heavily weighed their personal circumstances as reasons for why they could or could not take risks at different points in their careers. They credited finances, education, mentors, and familial support as huge motivators in taking a leap of faith, despite the risk involved. If these things were in line, creating a "safety net" of sorts, taking a risk was more feasible.

In fact, it seems that across the board, a safety net for the InnovateHERs often looked like finding quality mentorship, building a financial cushion, or enlisting familial support. Those who didn't have a safety net defaulted to hard work, a do-anything attitude, and persistence. Several also mentioned postponing starting a family so that they could see their personal missions become a reality.

This tension between what externals factors influence a person's risk acceptance is important to research further. Our interviews make clear that privilege—educational, socioeconomic, racial—does clear the path for many women to take risks. However, the absence of privilege leads to the development of other skills, including persistence, the ability to navigate a limited structure, and independence—all of which also serve as important factors in success and an entrepreneurial mindset.

In addition to talking about mitigating risk on a personal level, the InnovateHERs discussed what calculated risk-taking looks like when building an organization. They referenced the importance of making great hires to diversify their teams' strengths, creating strategic partnerships, and assembling a board with different perspectives.

Certainly, each found their own special formula. Having a strategy for risk mitigation is an important step for any InnovateHER in building their product, service, or policy in purpose-driven sectors. Combined with a clear purpose and a reason for why the risk is worth taking, this can create a powerful formula for social change and success.

Sherrie and Vicky's stories underscore many of the lessons learned from our research at the University of Pennsylvania. Risk-taking isn't as much a strength for InnovateHERs as it is for entrepreneurs in general, and our research and interviews further reveal two key insights:

1. Empathy and optimism drive risk-taking in purpose-driven professionals.
2. Women can proactively mitigate risk by working to create their personal safety net in the form of mentorship, financial cushions, or hiring great teams.

Conversations about these two takeaways are especially important to have with women who view risk aversion as a weakness instead of a key component to leadership. As seen in both stories, risk-taking is invaluable if your mission is to instill real-world changes. Luckily, risk acceptance can be developed by applying the following tactics. First, identify your purpose for—and definition of—*why* you are doing what you are doing. Second, evaluate your personal circumstances and relationship with risk. Once you have mapped out your risk tolerance, it is crucial to reach out to a network and get support in your areas of weakness. Lastly, stay optimistic and focus on the potential that waiting on the other side of the risk at hand. As they say, "No risk, no reward."

Every InnovateHER we interviewed had their own risk journey of acceptance, but from the research, it is clear that not loving risk doesn't preclude you from being successful in the purpose-driven economy. In fact, by thinking about risk purposefully and proactively and by planning around it, your venture, organization, or project will have greater odds of success.

InnovateHER Bootcamp:

Using Calculated Risk, Optimism, and Empathy

Monica Valrani, CEO of Ladybird Nurseries

BACKGROUND

When Monica Valrani, the CEO of Ladybird Nurseries, first married, the expectation was that she would not work. In traditional families from India, it was rare for women to get a job once they were married. The difference was that Monica had studied in England and had been exposed to a different worldview. With a lifelong passion for education, she received the backing of her husband and her in-laws to get a certification in Montessori teaching right after moving to Dubai. Shortly thereafter, she worked as an early childhood teacher but decided to resign when she became a mother.

PROBLEM

Monica is naturally risk-averse. She had never owned a business, and she had spent the past seven years as a full-time mom. It made it that much more challenging to say "Yes!" when a friend called her with the opportunity to buy a local nursery. She knew in her heart that she wanted to do it—but the question was, should she? What would she tell her in-laws? Would it matter that she only had education experience and not business acumen? All the self-doubt and worries about taking a risk filled her mind. How could she create a safety net that would allow her to feel comfortable taking the risk?

LEVERAGING CALCULATED RISK-TAKING

Monica took a good, hard look at her resources. She knew she had the support of her husband, who offered to mentor her through the business part. The woman who currently owned the nursery was willing to onboard her. One teacher offered to walk her through the day-to-day operations from an education side. What would she do with her kids? Well, she could use this as an opportunity to be a role model for them! Taking account of all the support she had was enough to convince her. Even though it scared her deeply, she decided that the risk was worth it to go after a dream she'd had for years to build an early childhood center in Dubai. She accepted the opportunity.

APPLYING EMPATHY

To truly understand the business, Monica wanted to lean into her natural empathy. She took on every single job in the organization for a few weeks at a time to experience for herself how each person in the organization supported the mission. Her heart, always focused on the education side, was captured by the work they were doing in the classroom. She knew this was the core of the nursery. After doing the job herself, she knew also that to set the nursery apart from the competition, her teachers had to be exceptionally empathetic people, providing a special, personalized touch to each child and family.

BUILDING OPTIMISM

Early on, Monica had a split with a financial partner, and she decided from there on out that she wanted to surround herself only with optimistic people in the business. This experience, combined with the fact that risk-taking didn't come naturally to her, led her to look at risk from a different angle. Instead of asking, "What could go wrong?" she started to ask herself, "What could go right?"

"Before, I used to be more pessimistic. Surrounding myself by people who explore and look on the bright side of things has helped

me with my self-confidence and with my risk-taking abilities."
Throughout COVID-19, with the shutdowns of schools, deciding to
be optimistic was the motor that kept her going. She provided free
online services to parents who wanted them and kept her full staff
onboard and paid for a year.

OUTCOME

Monica's optimism throughout the COVID-19 crisis of 2020, her
empathy for her team, and her now set-in-stone risk-taking strategy helped her not only get through a challenging time but also
earned her loyalty from enough parents to expand. In 2022, she
will be opening the third major location of Ladybird with support
from the Knowledge Fund of Dubai. Ladybird's second location
has already received international accolades for its gorgeous and
environmentally friendly design and is the first US Green Building
Council LEED Certified nursery in the United Arab Emirates. Today,
Ladybird is ranked as the premier early childhood education brand
in Dubai, and between its three locations, Ladybird will serve over
400 children in 2022!

CHAPTER 6

Action Orientation + Idea Generation + Execution + Optimism

As investors and board members, we—Kathy and Bobbi—are constantly scanning the talent pool for new and exciting initiatives to support. We consult many intrapreneurs on their business and marketing strategies and work with entrepreneurs who have started their own companies or nonprofits. We've heard countless pitches and have had to give our fair share of tough rejections, but without a doubt, there is nothing harder and more deflating than hearing somebody talented pitch an idea and say, "It would be nice if...," or even worse, "We haven't done this because we are waiting for the perfect moment." As entrepreneurial leaders, we know that the perfect moment never comes. A common denominator for those whom we consult with, invest in, and mentor is a bias to action, or action orientation.

Action orientation is an essential trait for any entrepreneurial leader who is aiming to grow their initiative. The EMP defines *action orientation* as "a tendency to show initiative, make decisions quickly, and feel impatient for results."[2] Entrepreneurial leaders must be quick on their feet and responsive to their customers, especially in the early stages of starting a business or nonprofit. If they aren't, the competition is quick to jump on the opportunity to claim their customers. An entrepreneurial mindset—and action orientation, specifically—helps to scale new initiatives that are adaptive to their users' consistently changing needs. There is no waiting for tomorrow or hoping for a rule book to determine what to do and what not to do. People with an action orientation jump in and solve problems right away.

If you are reading this and can identify with the bias to action, then you might already know that bureaucratic institutions are not friendly to action-orientated people. They often don't last long as employees. Burnout is one of many symptoms of an action-oriented person in the wrong role—when they try to innovate and get hit with red tape and bureaucracy, a person who scores highly on this trait becomes discouraged. These individuals do best in organizations that value their energy, drive, and willingness to get their hands dirty. Individuals who have a strong action orientation trait thrive in an environment with few constraints and lots of possibilities.

Fascinating insights about action orientation emerged in our research at the University of Pennsylvania. We learned that while action orientation falls in the middle of the spectrum of traits for entrepreneurial, purpose-driven leaders, women outperform men in this trait by 19 percent. This is one of the largest gaps between the two genders we surveyed.

We asked whether this insight rang true to the InnovateHERs, and perhaps not surprisingly, it did. Action orientation was the second most self-reported strength after passion. The InnovateHERs who had founded their own organizations revealed that they are incredibly hands-on in driving operations forward. They felt taking action kept them on the cutting edge, involved in the business, and deeply integrated into pushing the organization's growth strategy.

The dangerous flipside to action orientation is erring on the side of going too fast, being too intense, or micromanaging. To avoid these pitfalls, we can think about action orientation as a seesaw. Leaders who strike a good balance between a bias to action and taking time for due diligence are few and far between. Surely, you can reflect on leaders that leaned too far in one direction or the other. Maybe it was a boss who made you do market research for a week and then never looked at the presentation, or conversely, someone who called a shot before consulting the team, leaving everyone to scramble and manage their time around a new deliverable. Either way, many of the women we interviewed agreed that action orientation is among the rare traits that could make or break an organization.

The stories in this chapter show how action orientation helped two talented women to launch exciting new purpose-driven companies.

Katie Fang's Story: An InnovateHER Always on the Move

Portrait of an InnovateHER: Action Orientation + Idea Generation + Execution

The first inkling that Katie Fang, the founder and CEO of SchooLinks, was destined to be an entrepreneur materialized at age 12. She made a bet with her parents that she would be accepted to an aerospace camp in Houston, Texas. While Katie's declaration would be bold for any teen, this one was especially ambitious because she wasn't an

American citizen. Originally from China, being accepted to this camp meant she would move to a country on the other side of the world, where she needed to apply for a visa, learn another language, and live independently. Privately, her parents laughed to themselves about her aspirations. Yet, as entrepreneurs themselves, they knew they needed to give her a chance. They half-jokingly agreed she could go if she handled all the paperwork on her own, thinking it was a safe bet because there was no way she would be able to follow through on such a complex process at the age of 12.

At the time, there wasn't a robust support system for Chinese students to study in the United States. This uncertainty and lack of structure didn't deter Katie. She was practically starting from scratch, but she was determined to make it happen. She had the idea, and she knew she needed to act quickly to get her paperwork in by the deadline. She dove right into the tedious application process and pulled together the required information that allowed her to be competitive for a student visa. When she finally got everything together, she took a deep breath and hit send on her application.

The joke was on Katie's parents! Bucking expectations, she was accepted to the program, and her visa was approved within a few weeks. What else could her parents do? They looked at each other, sighed, and gave her the nod of approval. From that day forward, she has been blazing her own path.

What makes Katie so special? Is the entrepreneurial spirit encoded into her DNA? Was her success a byproduct of having the right role models and resources to build these skills throughout the course of her life? The answer is that Katie's strengths lie in two sides of the entrepreneurial mindset: She has the personality trait of action orientation, and she has the unique skillset of idea generation and execution—or being able to dream big and then make things happen.

The EMP research suggests that about half of the work that goes into building an entrepreneurial mindset occurs when we are very young. The other half are skills and abilities that we develop as we grow older and mature into our adult selves. In other words, Katie had the Goldilocks conditions to become an entrepreneur—and when the right moment hit and opportunity struck, her action orientation personality trait meant that she was ready to run with it. She had enough positive reinforcement through her own entrepreneurial parents that it was almost a logical conclusion to start her own business when the opportunity presented itself years later.

Her experience at space camp was positive, and through the process of applying and going, she realized how important it was for her to become fluent in English. She spent the next several years traveling to different English-speaking countries and researching programs that would accept international students. She lived in Australia, England, the United States, and Canada before deciding that she would go to college at the University of British Columbia in Vancouver.

In college, she kept her grades high, joined many campus clubs, and was living the life of a typical university student. Although she was enjoying college life, she grew tired of the bureaucratic process of "box-checking" to earn a degree. So, when her parents called her to ask for a favor, she jumped on it. A family friend had heard about Katie's experience going abroad and wanted to do the same thing but didn't know where to begin. Katie gladly had the conversation with her, which led to another recommendation, and before she knew it, she was spending 20 hours a week working with Chinese students eager to travel and study abroad.

Almost immediately, Katie knew she was sitting on a business opportunity that could be a gold mine. However, she knew she didn't want to be solely responsible for guiding potential clients through this process each time, so she began to ask herself, "How can I automate this and pull all these resources together so that students can have an affordable, easy-to-access toolkit that breaks down the logistics of planning their futures?" From only $5,000 in savings, SchooLinks was born.

As it has evolved, SchooLinks has become a college and career readiness platform that leverages artificial intelligence to help students plan out their futures after high school graduation. With tools that support everything from course planning to standard examination preparation, it makes planning for the future easier for students and college counselors alike. Katie has steered the company through many pivots and has become an astute student of the market, users, and paying customers.

All her work and attention to detail has paid off. In June 2015, she was accepted into a competitive accelerator program that led to the growth of her business, and in 2018, she was named a Forbes 30 Under 30 founder—did we mention she's only 25? In 2020, despite an incredibly challenging environment for entrepreneurs, Katie soared over the obstacles.

When we asked about how SchooLinks performed during this tumultuous time, she exclaimed, "Well, it was definitely a great test of our grit, problem-solving skills, and ability to remain calm! We not only weathered the storm—we also completed Series A financing." With a team of 20 and growing quickly, SchooLinks is already profitable and has major plans for the future. Katie Fang is an exemplary InnovateHER who doesn't wait for permission, dreams big, and gets the job done. With another round of funding under her belt, she undoubtedly has a bright career ahead of her.

Action Orientation, Idea Generation, and Execution

Understanding how idea generation and execution interact with one another was an "Aha!" moment when creating the Portrait of an InnovateHER. We quickly identified that this interaction between the two skills as something that sets InnovateHERs apart from other leaders. The women we interviewed all had a certain energy and spark. There were many fun conversations, like Katie's, where the person being interviewed lingered on what had inspired them to start their business or organization and walked us through the iterations of their business models. This, in a nutshell, is the skill *idea generation*. The team at Eckerd College defines this as "the ability to generate multiple and novel ideas, and to find multiple approaches to achieving goals."[2]

In other words, this is the intangible energy that visionaries are known for. It is the possibility inherent in the question, "What if?"

Idea generation alone is insufficient for success, however, since it's one thing to generate ideas and another to turn them into a reality. That's where *execution* comes in—or "the ability to turn ideas into actionable plans."[2] While action orientation is the initiative to move ideas forward or the drive to get results, execution is the skill of turning ideas into tangible results. Many of the InnovateHERs had great ideas, but paying close attention to how they brought those ideas to life, and how quickly, was key in understanding the relationship between action orientation, idea generation, and execution. In Katie's case, we see key indicators of how an InnovateHER leverages this personality trait and combines it with learned skills to make her business into a reality. First, she recognized an opportunity. Then, she immediately assembled a small prototype. She realized the prospect for growth, had a few key pivots in the concept as she tested different ideas, and then once it clicked, she began to invest in her revenue-producing, scalable business model.

An InnovateHER strikes a balance between these three entrepreneurial skills and traits. You may recognize this balance in somebody who is constantly in motion. They want things done quickly, they are always looking to try something new, and they are easily excited by new opportunities. The difference between them and an idealist is that they *make things happen.* An InnovateHER with these traits moves quickly, recovers rapidly from failure, and is constantly pursuing her purpose. These traits are inherently accompanied by another important skill—optimism—which ties up the whole package of the mindset of an InnovateHER.

Ana Hidalgo's Story: A Better Future Can't Wait

Portrait of an InnovateHER: Action Orientation + Optimism

What are Ana Hidalgo's two biggest enemies? "Apathy and skepticism," she told us, without missing a beat. When Ana sees something that she doesn't like, she can't just accept it for what it is—she must improve it, and if it can't be improved, she'll create something new. Her journey to founding two purpose-driven businesses before the age of 32 comes from a place of impatience with the status quo. "There is just a lack of civic engagement in Ecuador," she explained, referring to her home country, "and with all the political and environmental challenges, we desperately need entrepreneurial solutions. We need doers who want to make a change."

Ana returned to Ecuador in 2013 after studying at the Harvard Graduate School of Education. When she moved back home and began to catch up with old friends, she couldn't believe what she was hearing. Even though the economic and political situation had grown worse, her friends had become more disengaged than ever. They talked about leaving the country, just when she had been excited to return.

She always knew her heart was in Ecuador and that her mission in life would be to fight for a better version of her country for her children. As soon as she returned, she began searching for a niche in the market that would allow her to improve the problems and challenges facing the country.

"For me, it's hard to see a problem and not to do something about it," she said with a sigh, shrugging her shoulders. "In my master's program, I received all this knowledge, but I just had to sit on my hands for a while before I could do something about it. When I got back to Ecuador, I got started right away on tackling problems that were interesting to me." With a new degree in hand, she began by asking the question, "How can we improve political engagement in Ecuador?" She quickly realized that many of the skills necessary to create civic engagement overlapped with the skills needed to become an entrepreneur. And that was when the idea for her first business, LAB XXI, began to percolate.

With Ecuador facing enormous economic development challenges, most young people were apprehensive, disengaged, and unwilling to step up to the leadership plate. Embracing her own drive, Ana developed a methodology to train teachers on how to teach these skills to their students using practical, hands-on projects. Her team observed a radical impact on the students who received the courses. Once they had a proven model, Ana approached the Ministry of Education to pilot it across the capital, Quito, in public schools. They recruited 15 schools and began to see results on a larger scale. Simultaneously, several companies got wind of what they were doing and began to ask for a corporate training program to develop social and emotional skills among company employees. The first two products of LAB XXI were officially on the market.

After a successful pilot, Ana expanded the model. Her core team recognized the need to broaden what was taught in LAB XXI to incorporate 21st-century skills, such as communication, assertiveness, planning, goal setting, and collaboration. Eventually, many of the programs evolved into courses that were oriented toward people seeking employment. Ana's action orientation led her to develop different products that addressed different problems and gaps in the market. She had a formula that she could iterate, and she did—launching an employment preparation program, a government-sponsored teaching training model, and a corporate employee training program in just a few short years.

LAB XXI has had resounding success across Ecuador. The team has grown to 24 people and has developed programs that leverage these skills to support a wide array of people, from high school dropouts to small business owners. They have built more robust entrepreneurship programs, leadership training, and a partnership network that includes Coca-Cola and UNICEF as implementation partners. With a growing team, a newly raised fund to continue growth, and increasing revenue each year, LAB XXI is clearly on a steady path to sustainability. With LAB XXI well on its way, Ana has shifted her focus to her new venture.

As Ana was building LAB XXI, she was also embarking on a parallel journey in her personal life: motherhood. Her daughter's birth inspired her to think about what kind of education she wanted for her own children—and her determination to be optimistic about the future began to further develop. She had already had great success with teaching the necessary life skills at LAB XXI, but sadly, as she began to tour schools with her husband, they saw that these skills were the antithesis of what was being offered in traditional schools across the country. That realization sparked another fire inside her.

Like many entrepreneurial leaders, Ana mentioned the importance of optimism and not letting perfectionism get in the way of progress. "It would be easy just to look at the problem with the educational system and wait for others to solve it. But I love to create, even if it's not perfect. Most of my ideas are versions of something I've read about or learned about and adapt to the local context. I see that we can solve problems in many ways, and I'm always trying multiple solutions. They don't have to stick. We just need to see what works best and run with it."

In September 2020, ReinventED Schools was born. It aims to be an affordable network of private schools across Ecuador that prioritizes a personalized education plan for every student based on their interests, needs, talents, and development. It focuses on the student as an individual, as well as the use of a relational education model that teaches students autonomy and ownership over the course of their educational journey. Ana has kept her social mission at the core of the business, with some schools costing as little as $40 a month per student. Using best practices from LAB XXI, the results have been promising—ReinventED Schools are disrupting the education space in Ecuador by keeping 21st-century skills at the heart of learning. Since its launch, they have raised enough money to expand and have already grown to three different campuses in Quito.

Being able to jump into action, execute an idea, and solve a problem was at the heart of Ana's mission. Her action orientation trait has been key to her success as an entrepreneurial leader in Ecuador's education space. Combined with a healthy dose of optimism, her action orientation shows us how ideation and creation can open a pathway to success in realizing the world you envision.

Lessons Learned from Action Orientation

Ana and Katie's stories are inspiring examples of how action orientation is a valuable trait for early-stage entrepreneurs. Both InnovateHERs have created comprehensive, scalable organizations, despite challenging times. They have both been led by purpose and optimism, with the aim to create a better world by building their own initiatives to meet their unique vision. These skills were incredibly important in getting their organizations off the ground. Our interviews touched also upon a contrasting question, however: Is there ever a time when action orientation can hinder an organization's growth?

In addition to demonstrating a strong bias to action themselves, it's important to note that the InnovateHERs rated action orientation as the #1 most important strength they valued in their team members.

When asked about it, they agreed that action orientation in team members becomes important as the team grows and as they step back from the daily operations. In theory, hiring for action orientation allows a leader to transition out of operational roles. In practice, however, few leaders with a trait of action orientation can do so. For our InnovateHERs, those who were successful in stepping back embraced their action orientation and channeled their energy towards the development of new products, adapting the strategy, and focusing on the big picture while their team barreled forward in implementation.

One of the women who best articulated this management strategy was Jamie Candee, the CEO of Edmentum. She started off by citing her own bias to action: "I like to innovate with constraints. Even as I set the vision and targets, I am careful about being too top-down. I empower my teams using tools like Agile software development and then give them the space to figure out the best way to get to the goal and try my best not to slow them down." Though she trusts her team to get the work done, she also understands her unique advantage and how to leverage her own action orientation in driving the strategy forward without being too overbearing. She constantly mentioned the importance of keeping empathy at the forefront to keep her teams motivated. Jamie shared, "You can lose yourself as an executive, or your team, if you don't figure out how to master the empathy part. We work on showing empathy and being relatable within the organization all the time, even if that's not something that's natural to us. I don't want a bunch of executives who think they're great and everyone should follow them. I want people who can make good decisions and sometimes make mistakes, but then learn from them and move on. That's what learning is about."

There were other women who cited their action orientation as a definitive barrier to sustaining and growing their organizations. In those cases, the leaders stepped down from a CEO role to focus on building new initiatives that stretched their optimism and idea generation skills. For others, being unable to transition from an early-stage growth role to a maintenance role was such a huge barrier that they left their organization entirely. Ana and Katie demonstrate how this skill can be leveraged so that InnovateHERs can continue to advance strategy from a high level, even as the company moves out of its early stage and transitions into a growth stage.

Undoubtedly, action orientation is a supremely exciting personality trait in the entrepreneurial mindset. Highly valued by investors, it is a golden ticket in the initial developmental stages of an organization or in turning one around. Our interviews revealed the following:

1. Action orientation is a highly prized trait for early-stage entrepreneurs and takes on an important role in hiring strategy when organizations begin to grow.
2. Combining optimism, idea generation, and execution, action-oriented leaders can be magnets for resources in the growth stage.

In our research at the University of Pennsylvania, we saw that action orientation was one of the top four traits demonstrated by leaders in the education, learning, and development sector. Women, specifically, scored 19 percent higher on action orientation than men did—one of the larger differences in the personality traits scale. This differential recalls Margaret Thatcher's famous quote, "If you want something said, ask a man; if you want something done, ask a woman." We know from our experience that women are exceptional catalysts and doers, and it is clearly a skill that sets InnovateHERs apart.

InnovateHER Bootcamp:

How Action Orientation, Optimism, Idea Generation and Execution Help Self-Directed Projects

Bobbi Kurshan and Kathy Hurley

BACKGROUND

As two accomplished women in the education sector, we—Bobbi and Kathy—have not only been friends for over 30 years but have had our fair share of challenges to overcome on our own path to leadership. Each year, we get together with a support group of amazing, purpose-driven women, and we talk through our struggles and our current projects. This group, in part, has been an inspiration for this book, but it has also served as a basis for our friendship.

PROBLEM

We wanted to write a book together that focused on the amazing accomplishments of the women we knew and that would explain why these women had risen to the top of their sectors. Additionally, we wanted to provide a model of success for future generations of InnovateHERs. As two action-oriented leaders, we dove into the challenge headfirst and began brainstorming a list of all the amazing women we knew. We had separate strengths: Bobbi was the researcher who took charge of the academic focus on the entrepreneurial mindset, while Kathy—a lifelong education executive and mentor—served as the networker who recognized that the barriers to success went far beyond mindset. As action-oriented leaders, we wanted to find a way to complement each other's respective visions of success.

LEVERAGING ACTION ORIENTATION

"Let's try it and see how it works" was the mantra for drafting the proposal of our book. To write a book, it is essential to be action oriented, because you have to go out and generate interest at the same time as you are writing. In our case, we knew that we didn't want to spend too much time conceptualizing, brainstorming, and structuring a book while creating our proposal. The real feedback would come from speaking to women, comparing their interviews to the data we had collected, and structuring their stories to show-case how their experiences correlated with our findings. We knew that as we went forward with the writing process, we would find undeniable common denominators among the women we inter-viewed, and through the different themes we identified, we would get the best real-time feedback. Rather than keep this process internal and discuss the interviews between just the two of us, we let our friends, colleagues, and team honestly review our work—and then we integrated that feedback into the final product.

APPLYING OPTIMISM

As our resident optimist, Kathy used her trademark optimism to inspire us to imagine what our book could become. In the moments when we weren't sure which direction to take, she reminded us of why we were writing this book and who it could positively im-pact. Her optimism played a crucial role in keeping us motivated throughout the yearlong process.

When deciding on who to interview, we immediately shared our contacts and got to work on connecting with a group of amazing women we have admired for many years. We were motivated by the idea that there could be more InnovateHERs out there and that telling these stories could inspire the next generation to launch purpose-driven careers—and together, we leveraged that to move the book proposal forward.

APPLYING IDEA GENERATION AND EXECUTION

True to our strengths, Bobbi was drawn to the big ideas. She loved the idea of writing a non-academic book—the first in her career—to validate the entrepreneurial traits and skills she had seen successful InnovateHERs demonstrate over time. Though she had thoroughly studied the entrepreneurial mindset in the "ivory tower of academia," she was excited to bring research to life and to a broader audience. The idea of connecting the dots between her own mindset and career, and linking that to the experiences of the impressive women she has met, was incredibly exciting. Her ability to connect the research to real people and put pen to paper was crucial in getting our drafts out the door.

OUTCOME

A dream team who got through the labor-intensive process of researching, interviewing, and writing to make InnovateHERs a reality!

CHAPTER 7

Turning Internal InhibitHERs into ActivateHERs

Think back to your first major promotion. Maybe you can still feel your heart racing and the smile on your face when you learned you'd been hired. Maybe it was something you had been hoping for, or maybe it was a surprise. No matter the reason, it felt *good*. It was validation of years of hard work and preparation. As rewarding as that feeling was, many of the women that we interviewed shared that it was fleeting.

Why?

By now, you've officially met the InnovateHER, and you know enough about her to know that on paper, she's a rock star. You know what entrepreneurial personality traits she was born with and what skills complement her personality to make her a strong leader—and possibly the founder of a purpose-driven organization. She may even seem destined for leadership. Surprisingly, however, many of the InnovateHERs we interviewed expressed the feeling that leadership was *not* predestined for them—it was something that they fought hard for. In fact, every single woman that we interviewed cited immense difficulties and struggles on the path to success. We call these struggles *InhibitHERs*. Understanding them was crucial to understanding our InnovateHERs. In fact, they were so pervasive throughout our interviews that we decided to dedicate an entire section to unpacking them.

InhibitHERs are the things that hold you back from success. Think of them as emergency brakes that automatically activate just as you are accelerating your career. At times, they manifest in the form of *internal* belief barriers—such as low self-confidence, being too much of a team player, or always wanting clear structure before taking a risk. Internal InhibitHERs exist inside you and are challenges that you have internalized from life experiences or the way you were raised. These InhibitHERs can be overcome, but it requires discipline and support networks to do so.

InnovateHER's Self-Identified Area for Improvement

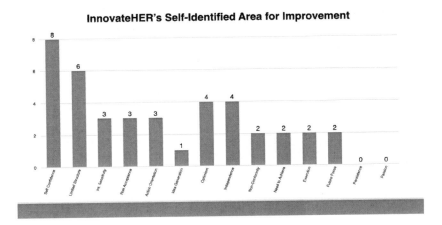

InhibitHERs can also be *external* barriers. These are the speed bumps along the road that slow you down on your path to success. External InhibitHERs are not within your control—someone else designed the road, and now it's up to you to figure out how to navigate accordingly and get to your destination on time with your vehicle intact. In Chapter 8, we will explain how external InhibitHERs are more present for women than for men—because in many ways, the path to success was designed for men, by men. We'll talk about which external InhibitHERs appeared the most and why women of color and/or women who came from families that immigrated to the United States have additional barriers that are important to understand.

Without InhibitHERs, we would not need to build entrepreneurial skills. In fact, the more InhibitHERs there are, the more entrepreneurial the leader must be. That, in a nutshell, is why we believe that women have developed so many entrepreneurial skills throughout the years and why they are so effective at navigating the barriers to purpose-driven work. Throughout the interview process, we heard time and time again about how the InnovateHERs learned to leverage different entrepreneurial skills to turn their InhibitHERs—internal or external—into *ActivateHERs*, or key lessons and takeaways that fueled their success.

We—Kathy and Bobbi—both experienced our fair share of InhibitHERs, both internal and external, on our paths to the top of purpose-driven organizations. It was a topic we were deeply curious about when designing our interview questions. Would we discover similar experiences across generations? Would new barriers come up, and would others be diminished with the passing of time?

While these struggles can be uncomfortable to discuss—failed boardroom presentations; a thousand no's before finally getting a yes; imposter syndrome; lack of funding; work-life balance, etc.—we also heard frequently that overcoming these barriers built character and tenacity.

The next chapters will discuss how each InnovateHER overcame her internal and external InhibitHERs by successfully converting them into ActivateHERs. You'll see that the way we unpack these stories is unique to each InnovateHER. Because there was so much diversity in the way each InnovateHERs' entrepreneurial traits and skills interacted, we thought each story warranted its own section to unpack the way this InnovateHER turned specific personality traits and skills into ActivateHERs to achieve success on her own terms.

Joysy John's Story: Navigating Self-Confidence and the Need to Achieve

"I believe in hard work above all else," said Joysy John firmly. She is the CEO of 01 Founders, a network of tuition-free coding schools operating in the United Kingdom—but her path there was not straightforward. "My work ethic, adaptability, and ability to problem-solve have gotten me through incredibly difficult situations. But the day that I woke up and physically could not bring myself to go to work, I knew I was in trouble. I knew that this time I couldn't get through on grit alone."

Hard work was a fundamental value instilled in Joysy from a young age. Grinning, she recounted an early instance of how she overcame weaknesses with consistent and deliberate practice. She remembered getting 40 percent on a math test in primary school and dreading her parents' response. But much to her surprise, when she handed over the exam results to her mother, she was met with a calm reaction. Her mother looked at it quietly for a few minutes, shrugged, and said, "That just means you need more practice. Let's look at what you got right, analyze what you got wrong, and work hard to fix it." Soon enough, 40s turned into 60s, and 60s turned into 80s, and 80s turned into 95s. Without realizing it, Joysy was building persistence, learning how to be optimistic, and slowly understanding that putting in twice the effort would pay off in results. From that moment forward, Joysy decided that hard work was her most valuable asset.

The value of hard work and persistence has served Joysy for many years. She has overcome remarkable barriers to be in the position she is in today. Relying on innate entrepreneurial traits like action orientation and the willingness to take a calculated risk, she spent her career working tirelessly to build skills that helped her to move countries three times, change industries five times, and rise to the top of the executive talent pool. Her belief that she could work her way out of anything was fundamental to her success. However, as she rose in the ranks of corporate and nonprofit organizations, she began to quietly worry if she was deserving of all the accolades. The more responsibility she gained at work, the more pressure she felt to work harder to live up to her titles—and to her own expectations. Without realizing it, an InhibitHER was growing inside her.

Here is the irony of this InhibitHER: As Joysy achieved career success, her confidence and optimism increasingly became tied to performance. When things were going well at work, Joysy felt great. When things weren't going so well, she developed a nagging sense of imposter syndrome—something she had always been able to power through in the past. She began to work longer and longer hours, relentlessly pushing herself to achieve more. She continued to hold herself 100 percent accountable for excellence, and her core skills—confidence, optimism, and even persistence—were called into question every time she felt that she wasn't living up to expectations. This all came to a head during her time leading the Education team at Nesta, an innovation foundation based in the UK.

In Joysy, the Nesta board had found the perfect leader for this purpose-driven organization. She was adaptable, action oriented, and independent—but also a great team player. She could get her hands dirty but also easily slip into the role of a visionary. Most importantly, she had a strong sense of empathy, and she could easily connect with stakeholders and with her team. They saw in her the entrepreneurial traits and skills of a leader capable of scaling research, innovation, and impact investment to take the organization to the next level.

However, Joysy didn't see those skills in herself, and her imposter syndrome grew so much that her first instinct was to *work harder*. She would spiral into cycles of worry that were harder and harder to break. Even though she had made it to the top, landed her dream job, and was leading a purpose-driven organization, she found herself paralyzed with worry, fear, and pessimism about her own abilities in key moments.

Fast forward to the morning when she could not get out of bed. She found herself lying there, staring at the ceiling, overwhelmed by the imposter syndrome InhibitHER. Her husband sat by her side, patiently waiting for her to speak. Recognizing that she, alone, could not work her way out of this was the first step she took toward truly stepping into her power.

For many InnovateHERs, this pivotal moment is the one in which you realize you aren't alone—and you aren't superwoman. (Well, you are, but you also realize superwoman had a huge production team behind her.)

Joysy began to address her internal InhibitHERs one by one. She confided in both her husband and mentor about the struggles and the sleepless nights. They advised against powering through this on her own and suggested she seek medical help. She started improving her physical health by exercising more, engaging with cognitive behavior therapy, practicing meditation, and using apps to support mindfulness. She also sat down with a work colleague and opened up about her anxiety and self-doubt. Much to her surprise, he had a similar story. He suggested she talk to more people, and as she had more conversations with leaders across sectors, she realized that mental health struggles were more common among employees in senior positions than she previously realized.

Joysy became braver and surer of herself after each conversation. She also began to set personal indicators of success, in addition to those she set for the organization. She was now using metrics that holistically took her well-being into account—including work, family, mental health, and physical health. Taking the time to redefine success allowed her to develop a plan to overcome her InhibitHER so she could successfully help her organization achieve its mission and bring her best self to the table.

Her network, her plan, and her actions became her ActivateHERs, and together, they paid off so well that she was recently named one of the Financial Times' Top 100 Black Asian Minority Ethnic leaders influencing the tech sector in the United Kingdom.[26] Since then, Joysy has joined 01 Founders as CEO, with the goal of building and scaling an entrepreneurial venture to address the digital skills gap in the UK.

Joysy's story teaches us the following:

1. Imposter syndrome doesn't necessarily disappear with promotions but talking to mentors about the issue helps to build confidence and move forward.

2. It is possible to recover from intense personal challenges and use the help received and lessons learned to reenergize career progress.

Mary Louise Cohen's Story: Managing a High Need to Achieve

Mary Louise Cohen is always ready to dive into a good conversation about her work. Her organization, Talent Beyond Boundaries, helps match displaced, skilled refugees with high-growth job opportunities on the global level, but her professional background is not in the nonprofit world. Mary Louise is a lawyer and has built a successful career in Washington, DC doing political and legislative work. She's incredibly accomplished, which made it that much more shocking when we received her EMP self-evaluation and saw that she marked "self-confidence" as the greatest area for self-improvement. We thought to ourselves, "If Mary Louise isn't confident, then who is?" Her credentials are enviable, and her resume reads like a checklist of the major movers and shakers in Washington, DC—including think tanks, nonprofits, law firms, and politicians' offices. We were so surprised by her self-evaluation that within the first five minutes of our interview, Kathy asked the question that was on our minds: "Mary Louise, do you *really* struggle with self-confidence?"

She threw back her head and laughed. "Yes! But it's complicated," she explained. "At this point in my career, I feel confident in my professional domain. I can speak to you two for hours about legal issues or about statistics having to do with refugee job placement, but I couldn't do the same thing at a party with people I don't know. I can't imagine, like my husband, going up to a strange person at the bar, slapping them on the back, and telling them a joke. I need to start in my territory first." In so many words, Mary Louise wants to feel confident in what she is saying before she can engage with others. While puzzling for someone of her background and accomplishments, this is remarkably common for women—the need to feel like an expert *before* speaking up.

Time and again, the InnovateHERs echoed the sentiment that they felt the need to be 100 percent prepared before going into a new job opportunity or launching a new initiative. While their male counterparts had the option to arrive much less prepared and manage the room in a casual and fun way, many of the InnovateHERs—especially the younger ones—said they couldn't imagine doing that. Self-confidence was the #1 self-reported skill that InnovateHERs wanted to improve. Not surprisingly, our research highlighted this gap in confidence between men and women—of the 124 educational leaders who took the EMP for our research at the University of Pennsylvania, self-confidence appeared as the second lowest entrepreneurial skill for women. Men, however, scored over 10 percentage points higher than women on self-confidence.

This finding tracks with research done over many years that confirms and documents the self-confidence gap between men and women. Most recently, a 2021 study published in the *International Journal of Environmental Research and Public Health* showed that women were more likely to self-report worse performance on math and science tests than men—even when their scores were the same as the men's. Even more disturbingly, the researchers were able to replicate these results with 10,000 middle and high school students, suggesting that self-confidence (or a lack thereof) is a skill that is reinforced from an early age and has a strong correlation to gender.[27]

Why do women lack self-confidence in greater numbers than men? Our research revealed that women who have a strong need to achieve personality trait are more likely to think they need to be domain experts to voice their opinion, like Mary Louise. At the same time, they often genuinely believe themselves to be less prepared, as seen earlier in Joysy's story. Underscoring these observations is the study cited above from the *International Journal of Environmental Research and Public Health*, which shows this dynamic is likely to have been structurally reinforced by gender norms for years. Combined, these dynamics create a cycle where women over-prepare for new opportunities but are still afraid to self-promote out of fear of retaliation.

Furthermore, our research revealed that for purpose-driven leaders, the gap is wider than for typical entrepreneurs and corporate managers. Women working for purpose-driven organizations scored 14 percentage points higher than women entrepreneurs and corporate managers on the need to achieve trait, and they also scored 12 percentage points lower on self-confidence. As we saw in Chapter 4, InnovateHERs hold themselves to incredibly high standards, especially if their job or organization has a social impact. What we saw when discussing InhibitHERs was that women show a tendency to devalue their contributions, making it more difficult to feel successful and qualified for top leadership jobs.

This raises the question, "How do industry veterans respond to this dichotomy?" Today, more than 30 years into her successful career, Mary Louise has learned to leverage her domain expertise in a way that feels authentic and helps her build confidence. Instead of advocating for a fake-it-till-you-make-it approach, she believes in showing up with humility first and working through the discomfort by using questions to your advantage when you are still building self-confidence. One way to help you earn trust with your team and stakeholders is by being vulnerable enough to ask questions and listen deeply.

"When working to make an impact for a population that doesn't come from the same background as you, you need to reach out and admit you're there to learn. Then, you need to learn from them by soliciting and taking their advice. When my husband and I started Talent Beyond Boundaries, the people we were working with trusted us because we didn't pretend to be something we weren't, and we deeply value their input to this day. You need to learn from the experts and not assume you know it all just because you're a smart lawyer or because you've had a successful career."

This radical approach earned Mary Louise credibility both with the people she serves and with her team. Above all, it taught her that curiosity is disarming. As Mary Louise gained more trust from her stakeholders, Talent Beyond Boundaries refined the value proposition of what the organization offers to companies looking to hire skilled talent and has helped over 430 refugees on the path to securing a job and visa in a new country so that they can start rebuilding their lives.

By admitting she didn't know everything, Mary Louise turned her InhibitHER into an ActivateHER and learned the skills of questioning, listening, and observing. Those skills helped pave her way into being a more effective leader in an industry where she was not an "expert." According to Mary Louise, she gained the confidence to lead and grow her purpose-driven organization through the following ways:

1. Validating the skills she *did* have to build confidence when feeling insecure.
2. Acknowledging she didn't know everything while showing a genuine eagerness to learn from the stakeholders she was looking to serve.

Krishanti O'Mara Vignarajah's Story: Self-Confidence and Getting What You Want

Krishanti O'Mara Vignarajah, the CEO of the Lutheran Immigration and Refugee Service, spoke candidly about her drive to make a positive impact. She is an InnovateHER who has found her path in purpose-driven work, and she credits her draw toward purpose-driven work to her family's background.

Krishanti was born in Sri Lanka, and at just nine months old, the family fled the country after their ethnicity became a minority and political target. As a first-generation immigrant in the United States, she felt the drive to give back from a young age. She had an innate desire to build her own pathway while lifting others up along the way. But it wasn't that simple—throughout her career, she was always aware of others' perceptions of her background, studies, and experience. She had to work to build her self-confidence so that she could step into a role of influence and use her talents to make a positive social impact for generations to come.

Though Krishanti had Ivy League degrees, honors across the world's best universities, and a dream scholarship, self-confidence was a survival skill that took grit and patience to establish over the course of many years. She prepared herself to work in international policy by going to law school, working at McKinsey, and studying abroad as a Marshall Scholar. She could tackle difficult problems by wearing different hats and thinking creatively in a way that specialists could not. So, when Krishanti secured a dream job working as Senior Advisor under the Secretary of State, she finally felt that being in a position of influence in one of the worldliest administrations of our time was the role she was born for...right?

Not exactly—because InhibitHERs are tricky, internal concerns that aren't defeated by external factors. As a young policy advisor in the Obama Administration, Krishanti was often involved in policy meetings where the room was predominantly filled with older, White, male administration officials. They sometimes sought to dominate the conversations with their years of expertise and opinions. After reflecting on this experience, she said, "You know, it's a shame we even have to say this, but I'm always telling the young women I mentor that there will come a time where they will doubt their place at the table. It's usually when a man says something you said 20 minutes earlier—a little louder—and gets the praise for it." She remembered the position she was in and the unique point of view she brought to the table. This reinforced her self-confidence.

"This may be an unpopular view," Krishanti said with a grin on her face, "but I see striving to make an impact as a double-edged sword that can hurt you but that can also be a vehicle for building self-confidence. Maybe as women, our quest for perfection is the motivation for putting ourselves out there, even when the reception is negative. We just keep showing up. The meticulousness and drive for excellence keep us hungry, and along the way, we begin to stop taking the criticism as a barrier and start taking it as fuel. We become confident through the process of becoming successful." Inspired by her time in the White House and the skills she built in her role as a policy advisor, Krishanti made the bold decision to run for governor of Maryland.

She knew she was an underdog. As a young woman of color and new to politics, she understood the magnitude of what being elected would mean. It was a huge risk exposing herself to national attention and criticism. But having sat at far too many decision-making tables that lacked diversity in opinion, race, gender, political affiliation, and other important identities, she knew the purpose of what she wanted to achieve was worth the discomfort of stepping into the limelight. She wanted to give back to her community, and no InhibitHER was going to stop her.

Running for office meant putting herself out there over and over again. Even as she performed well in the debates and received praise in the press and from friends, she still struggled not to harp on areas of improvement in her performance and the things she could have said. Even after a reporter from the *Baltimore Sun* named her the winner of the debate, she was surprised because she knew it was far from her best performance. When she walked off the stage and received effusive compliments, she would sheepishly say, "I appreciate it, but you don't need to coddle me." As the race advanced, she began to realize something: The numbers were telling her a different story than she was telling herself.

Being a data-driven person, Krishanti used polling data and an objective analysis of the numbers to turn her InhibitHER into an ActivateHER. She turned to pre- and post-debate surveys from audience members to gauge her performance. But she also drew a firm line in the sand not to let the information become all-consuming. By being focused and numbers-oriented, she now had an objective assessment metric rather than her subjective self-assessment.

Though she did not win the governorship, running for office was a deeply life-changing learning experience. She saw many positive indicators that the election had been a success: by being a fresh new candidate, by seeing high voter turnout, and by tying for third in a field of nine despite being significantly outspent by most of her male opponents. After the experience of running for governor, she began to explore what to do next. When she was approached to be the CEO of the Lutheran Immigration and Refugee Service (LIRS), she viewed it as a new challenge and, more importantly, a new opportunity for her to give back on an issue that had touched her own life.

Krishanti now leads a large staff of 250 people who work tirelessly to protect and embrace refugees, immigrants, and children seeking a new life in America—just like her family did so many years ago. As the leader of LIRS, she applies valuable lessons learned about grit and self-confidence to help lead initiatives that support immigrant families as they acclimate to their new home country. Her story reveals two notable insights:

1. When you feel you didn't do your best, don't expect yourself to be objective in reaching a conclusion. Seek out external data like survey data or hard facts. The facts can help you reach a more objective conclusion.
2. Recognize that having weaknesses is normal and acceptable. Practice the art of giving yourself grace.

Megan Harney's Story: Managing High Interpersonal Sensitivity and High Independence

Being an independent entrepreneur comes naturally to Megan Harney, founder and CEO of MIDAS Education, an education technology company that implements competency-based learning programs at scale. However, for the first eight years of the business, Megan preferred to do the operational work. She knew how to code, manage clients, and run the financial models. However, like many entrepreneurs, she learned she could not grow her business and do it all herself. When an investor told her it was time to hire someone, she knew she had to expand and empower her team. However, she had an InhibitHER: the struggle to let go of her independence and develop trusting relationships with those who could help her take her business to the next level.

Even as a child, trusting others was a process for Megan. She was bullied as a young child and built a strong sense of independence because of it. She preferred to spend time with adults discussing ideas and learning from those she considered older and wiser rather than play with those her age. She had been burned, and her reaction was to build a tough stance so that others would take her seriously. Her strongest skills are independence and persistence, two strengths she directly relates back to having gone through the elementary school playground roughhousing. At the same time, her experience had also formed a deep sensitivity to others' plights, and as an entrepreneur, it led to her wanting to see the best in others. She struggled with trust, but she grew her company with advisors and her own skills.

When her clients' needs began to grow and more districts purchased the MIDAS platform, Megan was nervous but excited to begin hiring. Her first big hire was a technical lead because she needed someone with stellar technical experience who could assume that role, freeing her to focus on expansion and growth. On paper, one of the first technical candidates to come across her desk seemed to be a perfect fit. Unfortunately, after a few short weeks, red flags started popping up—a lack of transparency, long response times, and sketchy coding. She hired someone she thought she could trust, but soon it became clear that this person's behavior could quickly sabotage the business.

After a few nasty interactions with this employee, it was obvious that though perhaps a technical fit was there, an ethical one was not. Much to Megan's dismay, the damage was already done. After consulting with trusted advisors, she decided to immediately cut ties with the employee. Legal action ensued, and the emotional rollercoaster of rebuilding began. It was an opportunity for Megan to look beyond the resume and the checkboxes to see the person behind the qualifications. Instead of shutting down and not hiring anyone, she used it as a learning experience to create a better hiring filter. It was an opportunity to turn an InhibitHER into an ActivateHER.

Megan learned a hard lesson. She took a few months to reevaluate what had gone wrong and then shifted MIDAS's hiring strategy to focus on a small group of independent and technically minded individuals who shared the values of kindness and respect. She knew that connecting with this small group would make it easier to build trust and empathy and that she would be more willing to invest in the well-being of everyone on the team. While it took time for her to learn to trust her employees again, once she did, the business began to grow alongside her team. She now screens potential employees for MIDAS Education's core values and takes these traits just as seriously as she does their technical competencies. She recognizes that *who* is on her team is just as important as *what* they can do from a technical perspective.

Because Megan is very clear about the hiring requirements for her company, she now operates with greater confidence. She takes good care of her team and invests deeply in them as professionals because she knows and cares about them. Her hiring strategy is intentional. Additionally, building an agile team aligned with the values of the business has allowed her to take risks that a larger team would not have afforded her. The trust she has with her A-team means that her leadership style is much more collaborative, and she rarely makes a judgment call without asking for their opinions. If she were to disappear tomorrow, she knows MIDAS would be in good hands.

For MIDAS Education, nailing the hiring strategy meant significant revenue growth. It meant they could pursue a riskier business strategy of only accepting a few big, government clients and several large school districts. Megan can afford to take the risk because she knows she can rely on her team to provide top-notch service to a small group of clients and follow through 100 percent of the time. By building core values and a hiring strategy around those values, Megan has turned her InhibitHER—a struggle to balance trust and empathy for others—into an ActivateHER that has helped her build processes to overcome adversity. She now can delegate things she never imagined she could let go. Fundamentally, Megan's strategy shows that bigger isn't necessarily better. Her experience demonstrates the importance of two key points:

1. Developing organizational values to affirm a hiring strategy that promotes empathy within boundaries.
2. Understanding that bigger isn't always better. If you're more independent-minded and you must work to cultivate empathy, then surrounding yourself with fewer people that you deeply trust is a valid growth strategy.

Silver McDonald's Story: Empathy Expands with Adversity

"Oh, no! I would never have thought of selling my shares in the first startup I worked for. It didn't matter how much I stood to gain personally—between youth and naivete, we had a culture and storyline that would have been a signal that I didn't believe in the company. I could have never considered doing that to my friends," Silver McDonald, now the Vice President of Growth at Hazel Health, said while reflecting on her first startup job. This level of empathy is unmistakable to anyone who knows her. She falls on the opposite side of the spectrum of traditional, self-motivated leaders. Rather than having a go-at-it-alone mentality, she has chosen to build her career using a team-centered approach allowing her to collaborate while also using strategic insights and customer relationships to drive her decisions. She focuses on building a long-term business instead of what provides her a personal win. Her EMP profile aligns with an InnovateHER.

"I feel weird saying this," she said, "but my interpersonal sensitivity has always been really high. I can walk into a room and read it almost instantly." She attributes this skill to the adversity she faced in early childhood. Silver lost both of her parents before the age of 16 and became a ward of the court—moving frequently between foster homes, observing, and adapting along the way. Additionally, as a red-headed girl named Silver who was 5-foot-11, she was an easy target for bullying in her early years. Because of this bullying, Silver established resilience at a young age—and even the wherewithal to feel empathy for her bullies. As she aged, she came to recognize empathy as not only a tool for survival but also a superpower. Instead of shutting down, Silver chose to open up to understand the culture, motivations, and social cues of those around her so that she could better adapt to her environment while also developing a strong sense of self at a young age. Empathy became her way of connecting with others, and it helped her assimilate in the midst of so much chaos.

After a tumultuous childhood, Silver's first job out of college was at a small, two-person company that was quickly acquired by the slightly larger visionary group, Razorfish. Her very first role was that of team leader. In that role, Silver did what she always did—she helped to develop the company culture and built cross-functional team relationships, earning the trust and loyalty of new colleagues and clients. Once again, she latched onto empathy and social connection as survival skills. That risk paid off, and her entrepreneurial skill of empathy helped her move to the next level in her career.

Silver rose through the ranks and saw the company grow from 30 people to 2,000 within two years. With a team of people, all under the age of 30, they built a tight-knit culture led by connection, collaboration, innovation, and passion to bring brands into the digital era. After six industry-leading years, incredible organizational success, and developing lifelong friends, she began to personally long for something more. She wanted to give back to her community and match her talents with her desire to help others. She was also feeling the telltale signs of burnout.

It was time for a pause.

Without realizing it, Silver's extraordinary empathy for others was on track to becoming an InhibitHER. She had focused on what was best for her friends and colleagues but hadn't stopped to examine what was best for herself. It was time to break that pattern. After some soul-searching, it became clear to her that whatever she did next would be in the social impact space. She began reaching out to a small group of friends and mentors. The more she shared how much she wanted to be immersed in purpose-driven work, the more people responded to her. Opportunities began to flow from the relationships she had previously built, but the difference was that Silver had defined her own motivations and was determined to set her own path. This led her to join another startup, Schoolnet, where she stayed the next decade, and to start a strong career in EdTech, as she combined the best practices across technology, consulting, and education to impact student learning.

A running theme began to appear in the challenges Silver accepted: She was recurrently being asked to rebuild collapsing teams, even whole departments, while developing solutions to new industry challenges. Perhaps the best example of this theme was at LEGO Education. When she was first hired as GM of the US and as part of the global leadership team, the US team's motivation and satisfaction were low. "How will these people make an impact," she thought to herself, "if they don't enjoy coming to work every day, if they are not aligned around the needs of our district customers, and if they don't trust the people they work with?" An employee feedback report ended up being an exercise in benchmarking because three years later, when she left the company, her team had the highest scores and was a top-performing team in LEGO Education.

When asked what she did to turn the team around, she said, "Empathy has to be balanced with organizational strategy, execution, and achievement. I focused on customer orientation, team development, and getting people into the right roles to be successful. I spent hours talking to them, guiding them, and helping them find positions that matched their talents and career goals. Helping people be successful and thrive is one of the things I'm most proud of [during my time] at LEGO Education."

For Silver, empathy is clearly a guiding strategy to being a good leader, but it is also key in the line of work she chose. There is a bigger purpose to every company she has chosen to work with, and she uses her empathetic abilities to build teams and to hire people who want to make an impact—all while keeping her own motivations and purpose at the center. "Purpose is the binding force when things get difficult," she said, crediting it as what keeps her teams on track and focused. According to Silver, it's essential to any team-building strategy. Strategy, empathy, and collaboration helped her team achieve that purpose.

Our research at the University of Pennsylvania aligns very closely with Silver's profile. It suggests that purpose-driven entrepreneurs have a more developed empathy scale than do regular entrepreneurs. Within the group of purpose-driven leaders, women score 14 percentage points higher than purpose-driven men on this trait. Throughout our interviews, we heard echoes of this data. The InnovateHERs referenced investing in the people who work with them, working collaboratively, and caring deeply about the well-being of their teams. In the professional world, people are taking notice. As seen in Silver's story, it was the secret to her success.

Silver has become something of a legend in the team building EdTech space. In her opinion, this is something that makes empathy unique in purpose-driven organizations. "I've worked with a number of amazing entrepreneurial people so laser focused on building this thing that's in their mind that they can completely miss something big happening in the room. This is understandable and why it is so important to have many forms of diversity across a leadership team. So having an empathetic leader in the room to complement that focus is crucial because if your people aren't okay, then your organization won't have the impact of its potential."

In her current role as the Vice President of Growth at Hazel Health, Silver is once again applying her skill of empathy to help a growth-stage startup expand. This time, the purpose-driven work is to ensure equitable access to physical and mental healthcare for all K–12 students and to prioritize the systemically underserved. While her external role focuses on expansion, her internal role has involved leveraging team members' diverse cultures, generations, and backgrounds to achieve the organization's mission—and yes, now she views company stock differently. Her experience teaches us the following lessons:

1. Having empathy for others is always a good thing—but it's just as important to be empathetic with *yourself*. It's okay to pause and ask yourself, "Where do *I* want my career to go?"
2. When a leader approaches their team with empathy, the team is likely to perform better by investing more time and energy into the mission of the organization.

Carol Ann Waugh's Story: Structuring an Entrepreneurial Pivot

Carol Ann Waugh watches the sun pour into her studio every morning as she sits down at her desk to start on the project of the day. You can find her there every single day, Monday to Friday, from 10:00 a.m. to 3:00 p.m. This is the timeframe that she works daily without taking a break. The structure has helped her make the transition from corporate schedules into the world of art and creativity. An entrepreneur by nature, she spent years running her own publishing companies and consulting with clients who kept a much more rigid schedule. The discipline and habits cultivated in that world have helped her transition to the role of a self-employed artist, instructor, and author—her latest entrepreneurial endeavor.

"The biggest shock for me about becoming an entrepreneur was realizing that I was not getting a salary!" she said with a sigh. "I had to go out and earn my own money, which was a big surprise at first. But I adapted quickly."

Carol's current working style bucks the stereotype that innovative and creative people are disorganized, unstructured, and undisciplined. It is also not a natural fit for entrepreneurs, who according to the

Entrepreneurial Mindset Profile®, prefer limited structure to more rigid working environments. What could have been an InhibitHER—a strong preference for structure—became an ActivateHER when Carol learned how to leverage it strategically to differentiate herself from her competition—and even monetize her skills. People knew where to find her, when to find her, and how to find her when they were looking to buy a book, take a workshop, or purchase a piece of her artwork. She responded quickly and succinctly and began to see her business soar as a result. Her savvy shows that if you have a high need for structure, you can use it in your favor to build a profitable business, too.

Carol was inclined toward entrepreneurship from an early age. After she received her MBA, she worked for Butterick Publishing, a publishing company marketing to the K–12 education market. This was the time she decided to write her first book, *The Patchwork Quilt & Design Coloring Book*, which became a best seller. In the early 1980s, she saw the future of technology and created the first-ever microcomputer directory of software companies and related associations and organizations. As the first of its kind, this directory quickly became a hot commodity, organizing the who's who of emerging computer and software industries. She loved the freedom of working for herself, but the growth was slow, and she didn't have the familial support that many entrepreneurs receive, so she decided to sell her company. Carol had been bitten by the entrepreneurial bug, though, and she knew that she would continue to innovate in her own way, in her own time.

After selling her first company, Carol spent a couple of years back in the corporate world. Being an entrepreneur at heart, she saw a need in the marketplace for a service to help purpose-driven technology companies to market their products to consumers. She couldn't wait for someone else to develop this service, so she left the security of the corporate world to start her own publishing and marketing company. Always the independent producer, she channeled her discipline and need for structure into client service by always showing up, turning in work, and being on time. She became one of the most sought-after consultants in the publishing and educational technology sector and built a solid reputation as an efficient and accountable producer.

After many years in the publishing and consultancy worlds, she thought she was ready for retirement—but what would retirement look like for her? While she was ready for a change, she wasn't ready to truly retire. She was ready to reinvent herself and find a new challenge that would be fulfilling and help others. Art entrepreneurship was certainly not on her radar at the start. She had no experience as an artist, and she hadn't fostered a long, latent dream of painting, sculpting, and crafting for a living. But one day, she remembered how she used to quilt. She decided to buy a sewing machine and get back to making something unique and personal, so she decided to take on the challenge of becoming a professional fiber artist.

Carol's ability to bring order to chaos was crucial, and it became the most important ActivateHER in her arsenal as she began a new business in the artistic community. Her discipline helped her sit down every day to learn a new skill—whether it was quilting, painting, or something else. She was starting from scratch, and without that internal structure, she doubts she would have gotten to where she is today. "I didn't know how to make art, but I knew how to make money," she said with a laugh, shaking her head. "So, I began by writing books as I was learning. I figured if I could simplify it enough to teach others, then I would really understand it, too. I also connected with a startup company called Craftsy and filmed three online courses with them. That gave me access to a worldwide audience." So, her art business began to soar.

Carol's preference for structure is a trend that is more attributed to women than to men. Oftentimes, it is seen as a barrier to entrepreneurship or innovation. People who like structure are often described as rigid, non-creative, and even bureaucratic. People embrace structure for a wide variety of reasons—a tumultuous childhood, concerns about financial stability, fear of failure, or simply finding peace in routine. Interestingly, when organizations hire a mix of people who do and do not prefer structure, magic can happen.

Unknowingly, Carol identified a real gap in the artistic community. "As an entrepreneur," Carol said, "you have to drive the business. You're the person with the vision. You're the only person who's going to make it happen." She realized that other artists had not recognized that. She found that they were often working many jobs in order to make a living and approaching their artwork in a disorganized way. Even if they were better artists, they were selling less. They were thinking of themselves as artists, not entrepreneurs. Realizing that they needed help, Carol decided to leverage her structure and developed a curriculum to teach other artists how to market and sell their art—taking her InhibitHER to the next level by turning it into an ActivateHER *with* an additional revenue stream.

Her commitment to structuring her time, courses, and business model has allowed Carol to write five books, run countless in-person and online workshops for quilters and fiber artists, and produce her own art throughout the year. She overcame the financial burdens and fears of starting her own business by using self-discipline to make the work happen daily. Carol had a unique approach to structured entrepreneurship. Whereas being rigid can sometimes be regarded as negative, Carol learned how to leverage it for her own benefit. Preferring structure didn't preclude her from being successful—in fact, it became her competitive advantage that helped her build a large client base and brought the reach of her impact to the next level. Her story reveals these takeaways:

1. Wanting structure can be seen as a negative thing for entrepreneurs, but it can be helpful as a solo entrepreneur when you are getting your business off the ground.
2. Savvy InnovateHERs in the purpose-driven space can reframe their preference for structure from a "weakness" to a value-add in chaotic organizations.

Internal InhibitHERs are incredibly tricky to overcome alone. They exist because, as women, we've internalized negative messages about our abilities, faced unfair situations, or have been conditioned to perceive our success in a certain way. We also heard that the burden of imposter syndrome occurs more frequently for women of color or who come from underrepresented communities, because they are less represented in leadership positions. It is essential to share that these challenges don't preclude us from leading organizations. In fact, we believe that overcoming them is part of what prepares women for leadership roles.

As we saw not only in Joysy John's story but throughout all the interviews we conducted, one of the most challenging InhibitHERs that InnovateHERs faced was some version of imposter syndrome. We learned that women use curiosity, objective feedback, and a network of support as powerful antidotes to the lack of self-confidence that leads you to doubt that you are "ready" to step into a leadership role. Additional practices, like celebrating their own wins and validating what they did know, helped the InnovateHERs to build up the confidence in themselves that they were qualified for their roles.

We admire those who spoke up about this InhibitHER because the more we discuss it and acknowledge it as a part of a high-growth career trajectory, the more we will realize we aren't alone. That recognition doesn't mean we should accept imposter syndrome as normal—we should not. But by bringing it to light, we can ensure future InnovateHERs don't feel alone and are encouraged to discuss solutions that equip us to create a world in which more women feel capable, deserving of, and represented in senior leadership roles.

We also saw how empathy can be both an ActivateHER and an InhibitHER. When it is turned into an asset, stories such as Silver's and Megan's shine. Learning to develop a healthy empathy with teams and stakeholders is a crucial skill for any InnovateHER looking to make a positive social impact. Women who identify as highly empathetic have a competitive advantage, especially in leadership positions—and the more we see this contribute to success in business, the more widely it will be accepted and recognized as an important leadership trait.

As we work to grapple with difficult realities, sharing our stories lifts the burden from us. The stories in this chapter teach us that turning your InhibitHERs into ActivateHERs can be incredibly compelling career boosters. What is certain is that, in the process of sharing and listening to others' stories, we become more and more prepared to be honest and authentic leaders of organizations making a difference. Having internal InhibitHERs doesn't make us weak—it makes us *human*—and overcoming them promotes the opportunity to develop empathy, wisdom, and both personal and professional success.

CHAPTER 8

Turning External InhibitHERs into ActivateHERs

In a perfect world, all the barriers to InnovateHERs' success would be internal, and nothing would stand in our way. If that were the case, challenges would be easier to fix because they would all be within our control. Unfortunately, the world is not something over which we can exercise control. As long as women are a minority in leadership positions, they will continue to face obstacles that their male counterparts do not. These external InhibitHERs are speed bumps on our road to success, and as we learned in our interviews and saw throughout our careers, not all roads look the same.

A crucial and hard truth emerges from this chapter: There are obstacles in the workforce that we simply cannot control or change, and they often directly impact our success and well-being. However, learning about these external InhibitHERs can make us better leaders, innovators, and mentors. **External InhibitHERs are real, and they are an additional barrier that women must overcome to get to the same place as men in their careers.** Whether it's growing up in a low-income household, having to face structural racism head on at a young age, or not being able to count on familial support in your career, it is true that not all women have the same number of hurdles to jump over. However, as you'll read about in these stories, these external InhibitHERs often became a powerful incentive to seek out purpose-driven work.

The more external InhibitHERs our InnovateHERs faced, the fiercer they became in their advocacy for a more just and equal world.

The women we spoke with noted the following as the three most common external InhibitHERs: a lack of funding for women-led ventures, a lack of representation in leadership, and a background of an underprivileged or underrepresented community in high-growth trajectory career paths. Simply put, external InhibitHERs are a part of structural problems that we must work to address to create a more equitable playing field for the next generation. These women demonstrate that, even though it is difficult, there are ways to address and overcome these challenges, turning them into ActivateHERs that boost you to the next level in your career.

Lezli Baskerville's Story: Embracing *Ubuntu* and Exploring Independence and Interdependence

Lezli Baskerville, the CEO of the National Association for Equal Opportunity in Higher Education (NAFEO), has overcome many external InhibitHERs in her career. Lezli explains the differences in internal and external InhibitHERs by comparing them to independence and interdependence. During our interview, she said, "Central to overcoming struggle is understanding your individual blessings and core values, such as to walk humbly with God, do justice, and love kindness. It also requires understanding the role you, as an independent individual, play in humanity while acknowledging the interdependence of humankind. There is a South African word, *Ubuntu*, that reflects our interconnectivity. It means 'humanity to others.' Ubuntu is frequently used to depict our interdependence, urging people to understand, 'I am who I am because of who you are.'

"When we want to create a better world, we cannot let external barriers bar our coming together as one on important matters. We must start by acknowledging our own strengths and weaknesses. Then, finding allies, we must create partnerships while still maintaining our own driving principles. This is the essence of independence and interdependence."

Lezli's understanding of independence and interdependence was the result of many life experiences. Born to parents who were deeply involved in economic and social justice movements, Lezli's life has been steeped in activism. Her father, a charter member of the Montclair Fair Housing Commission and of the Montclair Civil Rights Commission in New Jersey, gifted her and her twin sister books about struggles of people for "simple justice" worldwide. These books focused on the struggles of Africans on the African continent, in the diaspora, and Native Americans to complement what they were learning in school. Both sisters channeled his spirit and passion for social and economic justice into university and into their careers.

Lezli's pathway took her to Douglass College at Rutgers University, the nation's only public women's college. Being accepted into college was exciting, but it wasn't free—or even close to being affordable. To pay for her education, she worked three jobs. On top of those responsibilities, she was the President of the Black Student Union and took 31 credits per semester to complete a four-year curriculum in three years. As she excelled in academia and employment, she became acutely aware that Rutgers University, the flagship university of the state of New Jersey, did not reflect the richness of the diversity of the state. Why were the majority of her professors at a woman's college White men? Why were there so few Black, Latino, Asian, and Indigenous tenured professors and administrators at Douglass and throughout Rutgers University? Her activist roots did not let her look away. Determined to make a difference, she combined her independent judgment with the need to recruit others and build an interdependent team to create a plan of action and address these issues.

Lezli organized a group of students to disrupt the Final Four basketball game. Their goal was to do a sit-in and shut the game down until the university addressed the lack of diversity in the faculty. It was not her first time tackling a structural problem on a large scale, as she played a central role in shutting down Montclair High School for similar reasons. This time, it was on a much larger scale, but she knew that she and her team had what it would take to succeed in this effort at Douglass and Rutgers. She understood that the lack of representation could be an InhibitHER for her future success and would be an InhibitHER for other women.

The day of the sit-in, she was nervous but resolute in her decision. When the time came, she quietly walked down to the court alongside a group of allies with signs. Success! It only took a few minutes for the university to respond by offering a meeting with the president of the college. A few days later, when Lezli stepped into the president's office, she walked him step-by-step through the challenges with diversity and the negative impact that it was having on women and students of color. Shortly thereafter, she was offered a position on the president's selection committee for the dean of the college. Together, with the hiring committee, they brought on the first African American woman as Dean of Douglass, Dr. Jewel Plumber Cobb, who became a world-renowned biologist, leader in the field of skin cancer, distinguished professor, and champion for increasing the numbers of women and underrepresented minorities in STEM. Playing a leading role in getting Dr. Cobb to become Dean of Douglass College helped Lezli to better understand her power to see problems, speak up about them, and effectively work with others to solve them.

She understood in that moment that you don't need to share the same backgrounds or beliefs, but you do need to share a common vision and goal to work in a coalition with others. Their shared goal—that representation mattered—allowed her to build agreement, and by using her own self-confidence, persistence, and ability to execute, she leveraged the power of a diverse coalition to turn an external InhibitHER into an ActivateHER and gain crucial representation of Black voices in leadership at the college.

The lessons learned at Douglass led Lezli to take on leadership roles in the Free Angela Davis movement and to include preclearance and language provisions in the Voting Rights Act. It also led her to engage in the fight for fair housing, full employment, and equal employment opportunity movements, and finally, to prod states with dual public higher education systems to invest comparably in their historically Black colleges and universities as they do in their historically White colleges and universities. She was a part of a team that founded the National Congress of Political Black Women when the National Women's Political Caucus refused to accept into nomination the name of former Congresswoman Shirley Chisholm as a vice presidential nominee in 1984. All this experience shored up her status as a fierce advocate for justice and finally led her to become a constitutional justice attorney.

Lezli aligned her passion and her profession to work for some of the HBCUs, TCUs, and MSIs leading the charge on closing the education, employment, economic, wealth, health, sustainability, and justice gaps. Decades later, as the leader of the National Association for Equal Opportunity in Higher Education, Lezli leverages calculated risk-taking and action orientation to advocate for diverse students, administrators, faculty, and staff at HBCUs and other universities that educate disproportionate percentages of the growing populations of the nation and for underrepresented and under-served communities.

She is proud to be "fighting to move multitudes from the margins into the mainstream and upstream." She has now been doing this for decades with tremendous results. The NAFEO imprimatur is on every equal educational opportunity, inclusion, and diversity congressional legislation and education excellence, access, diversity, and success congressional appropriation of the 20th and 21st centuries. It's also on every federal and Supreme Court case in the arenas in which NAFEO has worked for 52 years and on legislation and appropriations of at least 18 states that maintain dual and unequal public higher education systems to this day. In 2020, the Black Lives Matter movement and the COVID-19 crisis—which bared for all to see the racial and ethnic healthcare and education disparities—led to the essential need for excellent, diverse professionals leading in the development and advancement of solutions, which Lezli feels proud to support through her work in education.

"The stars have aligned in this season of new hope. I am more optimistic, energized, knowledgeable than ever, and more greatly flanked by incredible, diverse colleagues. I am leveraging my entrepreneurial traits and legal talents, my individual blessings, core values, and understanding the role of my independence and the interdependence of humankind to achieve new victories." When presented with new challenges, she continues to demonstrate ways in which we can change external InhibitHERs to ActivateHERs:

1. Maintain independence; stay true to the values and the beliefs that brought us to purpose-driven work in the first place.
2. Look for allies who share our values and purpose to build an interdependent coalition.

Maia Sharpley's Story: Finding Funding to Level the Playing Field

Each time Maia Sharpley accomplishes a goal, experiences a great achievement, navigates a challenge, or gets knocked down, she closes her eyes and imagines she is wearing Wonder Woman's belt. Every challenge, whether successfully overcome or not, provides a valuable learning experience that becomes another tool to add to her toolbelt. She takes a deep breath, looks at the situation she is facing, and asks herself, "What new tool will I gain from this? How will that tool make me a better entrepreneur and leader in the future?" The path that leads to success is rarely ever straight—and that was the case for Maia. Looking back, she credits her optimism to being pushed to overcome the many barriers she faced along the way. Maia is often one of the few Black women in the room, if not the only one. As such, she understands the importance of her example for future generations. She chooses to greet the future with optimism—a learned skill that comes from overcoming external InhibitHERs.

Maia has always loved a good challenge. After graduating from business school, she decided to go straight into the highly competitive world of strategy management consulting. She was enticed by the intellectual challenge, the rigor of the profession, the chance to work with creative and brilliant teammates, and the opportunity to positively influence her clients. She loved thinking of new approaches, guiding others through the problem-solving process, and experiencing the gratification of seeing her clients featured in the news later on, attributing their success to applying her strategies. Eventually, the notoriously long hours and grueling travel schedule began to wear her down. As many women and men do in these situations, she began to ask, "Why am I doing what I'm doing? If I could choose anything, what would I be doing right now?"

The answer appeared in the form of an accidental meeting at a brunch. The people there were all in the world of education. Because Maia worked in a completely different sector, she had no idea who anyone was—she had just shown up at the casual invitation of a friend! She ended up sitting next to a retired Major General, and not just any Major General, but Marcelite Harris, who was the first African American woman to become general officer of the United States Air Force. As a fellow Black woman, she shared with Maia how much she had overcome to rise up through the ranks and earn the respect of her peers. Maia felt the confidence to share her story too—how she had struggled to get to the top of her game in the consulting world—and how she was unsure whether she wanted to continue the climb or do something with more meaning. She wanted a chance to seize the opportunity to gain valuable mentoring insight and advice. After brunch, they scheduled a follow-up lunch to discuss coaching and mentoring, which resulted in an offer from Maj. Gen. Harris for Maia to work with her at the New York City Department of Education (NYCDOE).

Serendipitously, that same week, she was also introduced to a former banker through another mentor, a woman for whom she had built a successful business plan. Unbeknownst to Maia, the former banker had joined the team of then-NYC Mayor Michael Bloomberg and then-NYCDOE Chancellor Joel Klein. After a causal yet open conversation with him at lunch, he asked her to meet another colleague for what she thought was simply an introduction to learn from a gentleman who had recently left management consulting to pursue his passion. This turned into an interview, and at the end of the meeting, she received a second offer to join the NYCDOE.

Two job offers within the same week to join the nation's largest school district seemed like kismet, and the scenario was intriguing. She decided it was worth serious consideration, so she jumped at the opportunity to join a team that had taken on the audacious task of reforming K–12 education from the inside. So began her journey into the world of government, policy, and education, where she found herself a founding member of the Children First team. As a newcomer to the sector, she had a lot to learn, but she actively sought the advice of experts, doing, "failing fast," and trying again. Her perspective from a management consulting background gave her the skills necessary not only to create, analyze, and improve upon existing strategies but also to lead the implementation of those new strategies.

As part of the major reform effort that the Children First team undertook, the NYCDOE had the challenge of integrating new strategies with existing processes and systems that supported over 1 million students. Maia led the charge in streamlining programs to create more efficient systems directly benefiting teachers and students. For example, she undertook the redesign, implementation, and administration of the department's complex high school enrollment process, which resulted in 89 percent of students receiving their top choice in the first year alone versus 47 percent receiving their top choice under the previous system, thereby bringing more equity and access to students—often from disadvantaged backgrounds—who had previously been overlooked.

As an outsider, Maia brought a new perspective, and working alongside the best and brightest NYCDOE educators and insiders helped her to understand how to put theories and strategies into practice. She leveraged her spark and business acumen to her advantage and began to earn respect within the department for her impressive ability to get things done.

Maia's journey through education took her from the public side of education at the NYCDOE to the private side of education when she joined Kaplan, a globally established leader in education. At Kaplan, she worked across all sub-sectors of education, utilizing her strategy and operations experience, building and running businesses around the world. Starting in Operations in Test Prep, she then built her first business—a leadership training organization—and soon found herself in the Asia Pacific market, where she helped expand the online higher education businesses, first in Australia and then for Asia Pacific. Her transition from building and running to helping others build and run businesses occurred when she ran the Kaplan Techstars Accelerator and managed Kaplan's EdTech portfolio. She then moved to the world of venture capital as a Partner at Learn Capital. This investment firm spans seed, early stage, and emerging growth companies dedicated to the transformation of learning and the improvement of individual and societal capacities, at scale.

After several years in each of those positions, she gained a clearer understanding of the landscape and what it would take to succeed. No matter where she landed, she saw that in aggregate, the same people were in charge—elite university graduates, most of whom were men, often surrounded with like-minded managers—thereby limiting the pathways and potential of others. Though diversity in education was better than in the management consulting world, she still felt she had more to do, and now, she had the skillset to do so. How could she build more inclusive teams that would give others a pathway to management and senior leadership positions? What barriers did others face on the way up, and how could she leverage her influence to help underrepresented managers get there as well?

"Growing up as an African American woman means you have to overcome a lot. You can either take anger or you can take strength from it. I choose to take strength, and I choose to adapt to the challenges. I recognize I am lucky as I have a team of mentors, men and women, helping me to get me to where I am. I also recognize that I am in a position to assist and influence the next generation of learners and leaders in the field." When she looks to the next generation, she looks to entrepreneurs who are working to make education accessible to more students because in her own life, education paved the path to better opportunities. After going through the corporate, public, private, and consulting sectors, Maia decided the time was right to make a big move—and with all the tools she had gathered in her toolbelt, she and her friend and colleague started a venture capital firm to invest in innovative technology-enabled education solutions, domestic and international, from Pre-K to Gray (adult learners).

As the co-founder and Managing Partner at Juvo Ventures, Maia faced a Herculean task. Juvo is an education investment firm that focuses on supporting technology-enabled education to unlock the potential of learners of all ages. She landed in a challenging profession where women—especially Black women—are underrepresented. An additional challenge is that education is an underfunded sector as well. The external InhibitHERs and obstacles were stacked against Maia and the firm's mission from the start, yet she knew her purpose lay in cracking this difficult problem. She also knew that to raise capital and source and win proprietary deals, she needed to put in double the work, double the "sweat equity," and be twice as good as everyone else.

As hard as it was, the time, effort, and risk paid off. In under a year, Juvo Ventures played an important role in leveling the playing field for education entrepreneurs across the board. By investing in companies that aim to increase affordability, accessibility, and educational outcomes for students, Maia made strategic investments that help learners gain access to high-quality education with tangible outcomes. For example, her investments in the early-stage diverse founders of Onramp, RideAlong, Eduvanz, New Campus, Talenya, LINCSpring, SchooLinks, and Ion, to name just a few, helped contribute to new, innovative ways to open doors of opportunity for learners from K–12 to adults. In her position, she positively influenced which entrepreneurs received funding and built a network around them to support their success. Like their peers in other industries, women leading education companies obtain a disproportionately tiny slice of overall investment capital. A 2020 EdSurge article cited that between 2 to 6 percent of women-led EdTech companies received venture capital funding dedicated to education, and disappointingly, the article states that percentage drops even lower to 0.32 percent for Latinx women and 0.0006 percent for Black women.[28]

This isn't because the capital doesn't exist. In 2018 alone, this same EdSurge article revealed that the total startup funding in the United States reached $150 billion, raised through 8,200 startup rounds. Out of the 575 unicorn startups—those valued at $1 billion or more—only four were education companies led by women. Across all sectors, women-led enterprises continue to be overlooked. Having lived this herself, Maia understands the problem and has built it into the ethos of all that she does. Now, as an EdTech ecosystem guru, Maia is on the cutting edge of making a difference in the education space, leveling the playing field for students, and representing women proudly wherever she goes. To turn the external InhibitHER of a lack of funding into an ActivateHER, she offered these recommendations to new entrepreneurs:

1.   Engage with mentors from an early stage. You never know which conversations will lead you to finding your purpose and next career move and pay it forward. Mentor others and help them on their journey.

2.   Trust your lived experience when you see an opportunity to make the world better. Don't be afraid to take a leap with the right team on your side because it can lead to more opportunities for those who come behind you.

Elissa Freiha's Story: Building a Network to Address Lack of Funding

Funding for women-led businesses is difficult in the United States, so when Elissa Freiha put the idea of beginning an angel investment network for women in the Middle East on the table at a family meeting, she was met with blank looks. The concept simply didn't exist. As a natural risk-taker, Elissa was excited by the challenge to shake things up to increase equality in opportunity and financial independence for women. Even though she was excited by the challenge, she knew she had a long road ahead of her.

Elissa grew up as a part of—and in between—two different worlds. Though her family was from the United Arab Emirates, she grew up in Paris and attended a series of American schools. She was immersed in French culture, receiving an American education, all while being raised in an Arab household. These myriad perspectives taught her how to walk in many different worlds at a young age and exposed her to ideas and opportunities her parents were never afforded. Adaptability and fierce independence ensued, and at the point of graduation, she was sure of one thing only: She wanted to be an entrepreneur.

After graduation, she sat down and began a list of possible business ventures. A nail salon? Too boring. A restaurant? Too high of a failure rate. On a late-night FaceTime with a friend who was working in New York, she shared her frustration; she wanted to start something, but she wanted it to have a purpose. What could it be? Her friend happened to be working in angel investing at the time and offered an option: They could start an angel investing network in their home city. They did a quick Google search and found that there were very few angel investing networks in Dubai, and none had a lens on gender. They decided to throw their idea at the wall and see if it would stick.

At the beginning, ironically, they knew their investors needed to be men. It wasn't long until they bumped up against the systemic sexism in the investment world. As two young women in their 20s, they were repeatedly dismissed by male investors, many of whom not only rejected their proposal but flat-out refused to hear it in the first place. Soon enough, they ran out of options. They regrouped and started wondering whether things would change if they shifted their focus to invest in women-led businesses that had positive social impact.

It was a great idea, and it immediately began to generate attention on a national and international scale. The entrepreneurial ecosystem in the Middle East desperately needed support, and much like in the US, women in the United Arab Emirates were receiving a measly fraction of the support and resources needed to get a thriving industry off the ground. The problem was the small market and the fact that the actual business model was difficult to conceptualize. Few people were interested in investing in this niche and emerging market, and it was difficult for people to take a risk on a vision that didn't align well with the country's culture. The business model Elissa launched for Womena failed—but she continued to receive positive feedback about the idea and purpose behind the business, so she persisted and found a new path, rather than giving up altogether.

Clearly, intrinsic biases and misperceptions about women-led or women-owned companies existed in Dubai. She had heard the real stories of success over the years, however, what women had overcome to start their own ventures and the positive impact they had made. So, Elissa took a step back and asked, "What if we drive the narrative, really own it, to dismantle these biases and perceptions?" Thus, Womena was reborn as a media company. Today, Womena is a media platform that shares the stories of women who are innovators, creatives, and changemakers from the Middle East with a global audience. They also built an in-house accelerator program to support the women entrepreneurs in their network, which ran for three years and was supported by Standard Chartered Bank, Boston Consulting Group, Laitham & Watkins Laws Firm, Google, and Facebook. Representing leading firms in the banking, legal, consulting, and tech sectors, these backers are quite remarkable.

As Elissa explained during our interview, "We urgently need to tell the story of these women because they aren't visible. And even for a person like me, who's worked in this industry for eight years, I still sometimes struggle to think of a high-achieving female role model that has done what I've done before in the Middle East. Even once you stray away from the conventional American 'celebrity' entrepreneurial models, there are even fewer examples in France, and even *fewer* examples in Lebanon or the UAE. But they do exist. What I do with Womena is just highlight the role models that already exist. They were already there paving the way forward long before I got here. I want to take back ownership of the stories being told about our region and about women in our region, and tell them in a non-Western-centric, non-male lens, so we can see their true power and understand their unique stories."

Womena is following a long-term strategy to grow and expand the business. The struggle to achieve financial independence is real, but this year, Womena has taken important steps in that direction by diversifying their clients and beginning to explore new revenue streams that relate back to their mission. One such decision they made was to discontinue the accelerator program. While it was successful, they have made the conscious decision to keep their focus on sustainable, high-growth initiatives. Elissa firmly believes that the root of entrepreneurship is understanding your client, and now, she is committed to providing a platform for women-owned brands in the Middle East that can best tell their stories and help them connect to and grow their audiences.

Elissa, much like Maia, recognized lack of funding as an external InhibitHER. That obstacle became an ActivateHER because it forced them into action to start their own companies. Although Elissa is 20 years Maia's junior, she can imagine a world in which she expands her media company into a global empire that shatters existing misconceptions and redefines the global understanding of women as changemakers. Her InhibitHERs—a still ripening entrepreneurial ecosystem, lack of funding, and systemic sexism—are not easily solved, but her experience provides valuable insights:

1. If systemic challenges stand in your way, it is important to know when to shift priorities and wait for the right time to push forward. You should never wait for the future to come to you.

2. Using creativity and flexibility, you can build a business or service to meet immediate needs while also developing relationships to help you achieve your long-term vision.

Rebecca Winthrop's Story: Applying Entrepreneurial Mindset as an Intrapreneur

On paper, Rebecca Winthrop, Co-Director of the Center for Universal Education at the Brookings Institution, is the ideal entrepreneur. Within the first few minutes of our interview, she brightly exclaimed, "I love building things!" She has a strong action orientation, little patience for bureaucracy, and loves to brainstorm new projects. Her weakness—and what she hires for—is execution of her vision, which she prefers to outsource to her team. Though this might check all the boxes of a typical entrepreneur, Rebecca is clear that starting her own company isn't in her plans.

"I never, ever, ever wanted to own my own business," she said. "My parents owned their own business, and they always struggled with money. I would see them pulling out their hair thinking about how we were going to pay for things between contracts and checks coming in. I always wanted more control." Rebecca made a conscious decision to seek more stability for herself and her family by not becoming an entrepreneur. The catch is that she was both born and raised with an entrepreneurial mindset—so what about her work environment makes it possible to thrive?

First, it's important to mention that Rebecca's entrepreneurial mindset is evident in everything she describes about her job. When she shared her favorite things about her position with us, she cited the freedom to make her own schedule, autonomy over her own budget, accountability for her own results, and the responsibility to seek out her program's own funding. Additionally, she spoke eloquently about how passion drives her work as an intrapreneur. She cited how frustrating it was to see the hypocrisy of colleagues doing social justice work when they had no clear purpose-driven mission. It was evident that she deeply valued building a team that shared her ambition for pursuing meaningful ideas and making them reality.

Second, while her family background deterred her from striking out on her own, it also suggests these entrepreneurial traits were built into her DNA. Rebecca's passion for helping others has taken her from being an intern at the International Rescue Committee to building out the IRC's global education practice and then to directing the center, leading all education initiatives globally at the Brookings Institution. Nevertheless, she has faced different challenges than founders do when launching a startup. Instead of focusing on building a customer base, she has had to become a fierce advocate for her projects and initiatives within the Brookings Institution. She has had to overcome bureaucracy and competing interests within the organization and navigate shifting institutional procedures.

Rebecca is better equipped than most to navigate those challenges, thanks to her entrepreneurial personality traits instilled in her by her parents and upbringing. In many cases, she has applied the same skills entrepreneurs have to different challenges and has been more persistent than a traditional corporate manager. As a rule of thumb, the bureaucracy and risk aversion in large nonprofits make innovation difficult within them. She learned how to channel her idea generation, need to achieve, and action orientation toward getting things done on a larger scale but slower timeline and how to make an effective case for external and internal resources to be dedicated to her projects.

Rebecca's personality traits have helped her attract resources, and she has grown her program from three to 50 team members; it is now one of the largest centers in the organization. In her words, she operates "a little nonprofit inside a bigger nonprofit," and she works with ample autonomy, independence, and freedom to implement innovative Brookings' initiatives in the education sector. Though she decided not to become an entrepreneur herself, she has found an organization that permits her to have the Goldilocks conditions for innovation along with the stability of a large organization. While she may never see the high returns that someone who decides to launch their own business may have, she will also never see the low lows that many entrepreneurs must face. For Rebecca, being an intrapreneur is ideal.

Of all the women interviewed for this book, 85 percent mentioned that their familial backgrounds have had some influence or significant influence on their decisions to go into purpose-driven work. Whether it was a negative experience that they were determined to make better, the example of a brave parent leading the way, or the values with which they were raised, purpose is modeled early on and can be an important motivator in difficult endeavors, as InnovateHERs often undertake. In Rebecca's story, we can see the circumstances in which she grew up being a powerful motivator not to start a business, but from having entrepreneurial parents, she also learned the gift of approaching problems entrepreneurially.

This story demonstrates what it means to use an entrepreneurial mindset to start and grow programs internally at a large organization and how to exercise your entrepreneurial spirit when you don't aim to start a company of your own. To grow as an InnovateHER within an organization, the organization itself must value the entrepreneurial mindset. In a place where you can make proposals, earn trust to build new initiatives, and be given the freedom to carry out your own projects, you can truly become an InnovateHER. While not wanting to be an entrepreneur could have been an InhibitHER, Rebecca turned it into an ActivateHER by using her entrepreneurial skills to become a leader in her organization and fulfill her personal goal of positively impacting others. Rebecca's experience reinforces key points about the entrepreneurial mindset:

1. You don't have to be an entrepreneur to be entrepreneurial.
2. If you have entrepreneurial characteristics but don't have the desire to start your own venture, you must look for organizations that value InnovateHER characteristics and use that as a platform to make an impact.

Jamie Candee's Story: Financial Restraints and the Impact of Female Role Models

Jamie Candee stood nervously at the back of the class in second grade. Would her teacher realize that she couldn't read? Or worse, would she make her read out loud? Jamie had been in speech therapy intermittently as a part of an individualized education plan in her public school. It was clear she had trouble processing information, but the IEP program lacked consistency, which made it twice as difficult to accurately diagnose her learning differences. The best option for Jamie's family was to work with the resources offered by her public school. While her parents were industrious and hard-working, private tutoring and evaluation services were expensive and out of reach. Looking back, as a second-grade student, she felt a little lost and unsure about how she would keep up with her peers.

Enter Mrs. Rubright, Jamie's second grade teacher. Before Mrs. Rubright, Jamie didn't think she could love reading. This teacher took the time to sit with her for months on end to figure out what was going on and to work with the school's speech therapist to find a plan that would work for her. Jamie was one of the lucky students who had someone believe in her enough to personally oversee her development throughout the entire school year. Not only did her reading skills improve, but by the end of the year, she was reading at a fifth-grade level. "As someone with learning differences, I realized the power of one educator who cares enough to really work with a child," Jamie said, her voice thick with emotion. "And that fundamentally changed the course of my life. I decided from early on that I was going to work as hard as I could to pay it back."

Many teachers go into education to make a difference in the lives of children. In Jamie's case, she lucked out over the years with a series of teachers who helped her work through her learning differences to ensure she kept up in class. Her father worked hard to provide for his family, went to night school to complete a college degree when Jamie was only six, and spent his career as a machinist and boiler operator.

Her mom worked as a stylist at her own small hair salon. Because both of her parents worked 12–14 hours a day, Jamie was often with her brother at their grandmother's house during the week. Though there was a lot of love in her house, she did not have the kind of additional familial resources she needed to get ahead. Most of her family graduated high school and immediately entered the workforce. Had Jamie chosen this path, it would have been perfectly acceptable. She was neither pressured nor expected to pursue a post-secondary education.

Without the influence of those teachers, Jamie questions whether she would have graduated high school. She also felt the weight of her parents' sacrifice. She saw how much aptitude they had, but because they hadn't continued in school, they were relegated to jobs that were below their skill level. She resolved to make them proud and to work hard to combine aptitude and a post-secondary education to pursue a career path worthy of her abilities. Her family situation no doubt fueled her innate need to achieve. Years later, as the CEO of Edmentum, she still uses the need to achieve to drive her success. In her words, "I'm achievement oriented. I operate off reaching goals because I grew up with a fear of losing things all the time. I know what it is like to see struggle, and I'm driven on some level by the need for security."

The traits and skills built growing up in a household with parents who had to use an entrepreneurial mindset to provide all the basics for their children are deeply relevant to the work she does today. When she got to high school, she already knew she wanted to go to college. She got a job detasseling corn at age 14 to begin saving money. When the time came to begin applying for schools, she fell right in the gap between qualifying for some financial aid but not enough to fully cover her living expenses. Nevertheless, she was determined to attend college and become a teacher. She enrolled in the University of Wisconsin-River Falls and began working in the summers, during the day, as a pre-school teacher. At night, she held shifts at two different restaurant jobs. Though she enjoyed being in the classroom, she realized she was obsessed with why things were done the way they were done in the classroom.

After speaking to advisors, she realized that she was more interested in education policy than in becoming an educator. The implications of this decision were huge—it would mean changing majors, aiming for law school, and above all else, a lot more debt. Was her passion worth it? The loan from her undergraduate degree was already crippling. She flashed back to the countless times she saw parents sitting quietly at the kitchen table after dark, staring at the bills, and decided to play it safe; she postponed the decision and opted to save up. She was offered a banking internship, which turned into a full-time job in financial services that helped her pay the bills. While the ability to pay the bills was great, she became disillusioned with the leadership at the institution, which created a deep dissatisfaction with her job—with her *purpose*. What had happened to the seven-year-old girl who wanted to be like Mrs. Rubright when she grew up?

Resolved to make her way back into education, she began to put out her feelers and go to education networking events. She knew she didn't have the resume to be picked from a recruiting pile, so she had to rely on her charm, instincts, and passion for education to get a job. Finally, she got a bite from the head of HR at PLATO Learning. In the early 2000s, she joined as an HR Manager in what was setting itself up to become one of the first fully online EdTech companies in the United States. In the absence of formal HR training, her entrepreneurial mindset helped her learn the position. She attributes her success to her calculated risk-taking, need to achieve, willingness to jump into action, and high levels of empathy. By the time she left the company (several years later), she had risen in the ranks to become Chief Operating Officer. It was at that time that her career took off on an exponential curve.

From leading a sale of Questar Assessment to the Education Testing Service to turning around multiple struggling education companies, Jamie has had her fair share of barriers and challenges to overcome. She has leaned into the skills she learned growing up— working hard for everything she's ever had, motivated by her parents' hard work—and the experiences she had with teachers to double down on her purpose. Now, as the CEO of Edmentum, she leads a team of over 1,500 education professionals, who serve educators and students in more than 40,000 schools throughout the United States. Jamie's story demonstrates that InhibitHERs such as financial constraints or learning differences can be turned into ActivateHERs. Her experiences reinforce the following:

1. Early childhood experiences and caring, committed role models—both inside and outside the home—are influential in defining one's purpose.
2. Risk acceptance is important to measure when following your purpose, and when the tradeoffs are too high, it's worthwhile to step back to find another path to achieve your purpose.

Jane Kubasik's Story: Giving Back—When Your Purpose-Driven Organization Is Personal

Taking risks wasn't always an option for Jane Kubasik. Born into a low-income family, neither of her parents had the opportunity to go to college. From a young age, she knew she would have to bootstrap her way to a college degree. Like many students, Jane was not afforded the luxury of exploring career paths that suited her personal interests. As a result, she picked her major in college after seeing multiple ads for accountants on a job board at her school. "If someone is hiring accountants, this will probably be a safe bet to pay back all of my student debt," she thought. She went all in, even though she would've loved more time to explore her interests. Unfortunately, at that point in time, going out on a limb to explore an unstable career path wasn't an option. She didn't have a safety net waiting to catch her, and like many in this situation, she made the safe choice.

Fortunately, her story doesn't end there. As years passed and she became more and more successful as an accountant, Jane realized that what she really enjoyed about her job was understanding what made businesses work across sectors. "When you work for a large public accounting firm, you start to see that a lot of businesses face the same types of challenges, no matter the sector. And when I started to have children of my own, I realized that many of those challenges also cross over into the education sector. I felt very strongly, and still feel to this day, that those two sectors [business and education] do not collaborate well together, and there is a huge opportunity to bridge the gap. That's when I started to find my purpose and to explore this as a career path."

Though it wasn't the most comfortable path to take, Jane knew she wanted to help students understand the relevancy of their school's curriculum to real-world, 21st-century careers. She declared it her personal mission to improve communication and collaboration between the education and business sectors. Wanting to bridge the two worlds, Jane started by joining the board of a small local nonprofit called the Montgomery County Business Roundtable for Education, which worked with public schools to improve students' college and career readiness. Her scrappy mindset paid off, and eventually, she was leading the organization. In this role, one of her main tasks was to lead a Young Professionals Conference event where businesses presented real-world problems for students to solve. They saw that the students were empowered, engaged, and excellent problem-solvers. Students cited the transformational nature of these projects and interactions. This rang especially true for children who came from families that were underrepresented in high-growth careers—the exposure to their career options and the opportunities to explore the skills necessary to be qualified for those jobs was life-changing.

After several years, Jane had an idea: What if they could scale this event and make it widely available? What would it look like to expose all students across the United States to the opportunities waiting for them? She shifted the organization into a national nonprofit, the 114th Partnership, which helps young people navigate education and career pathways by providing easy-to-implement, evidence-based programs related to high-growth, STEM-oriented careers.

"A big part of my way of thinking is scrappy," she said. "But just because a skill is innate doesn't mean you're good at it—you still have to develop it." She dove into the project with a drive to learn. This time, it was personal. Her own experience choosing a career for her future financial security highlights the importance of exposing young adults to different careers at earlier ages. Simply put, Jane and her team realized that many students weren't even aware of future career options, and the majority didn't understand how they could qualify for those jobs. The goal of the 114th Partnership was to prepare students so that, by the time they arrive at a post-secondary education program (college or otherwise), they would be equipped with a trove of professional experience that resonated with their own interests and talents. This preparation would enable them to be more effective in filtering out options that would lead them to high-growth trajectory career pathways.

Although it sounds like a simple decision, looking back, scaling this solution went against the risk-averse instincts she'd developed since childhood. Often, in the middle of the night, she'd wake up in a cold sweat thinking about everything that could go wrong. Despite the risk, she remained committed to her vision, which motivated her to press on. The team decided that the solution would be to convert this event into a tech-based platform of interactive videos—free and on-demand for educators—so that it could be accessed by any educator across the United States. The Spark 101 platform was born.

Since taking the plunge, Jane has relied on her strong work ethic and clear vision to build her dream. Jane and her team had achieved their goal of capturing a library of relevant challenges in the workplace and adapting it to become real-world, interactive challenges that allowed students to build relevant skills for the 21st-century workplace. Looking back, she sees it as a tool she would have wanted for herself when she was insecure about pursuing her interests and purpose.

In 2017, she stepped out of the leadership role, and in 2019, Spark 101 merged with a larger STEM nonprofit (Learning Undefeated), where it currently lives as a series of STEM skills videos presented by employers and free to educators.

Notably, at the time Jane started Spark 101, she and her husband had built a financial safety net that allowed her to take a risk and start a new venture. This theme recurred throughout our interviews—the women who had a financial safety net considered it an important factor in making the decision to strike out on a nontraditional path and start something new. For those who didn't have the comfort of a financial safety net, their success was a point of pride and a benchmark for how much they had achieved with little support. Financial security was an important decision-making factor in whether to start their own ventures or work for someone else, and even the most entrepreneurial women we interviewed looked for financial security before embracing risk.

Even with a financial safety net, Jane was determined to make Spark 101 the most successful EdTech product she could by using the business expertise and tools of board members to brutally evaluate potential risk and develop risk-mitigating strategies. The product had to be excellent—that was non-negotiable. She leveraged mentors and the board to develop Spark 101's content so that it was authentic for employers, educators, and students alike. Jane's risk paid off, and her determination to give back has given many young adults the opportunity to dream big. Her experience demonstrates the following:

1. It's okay if risk doesn't come naturally to you. It's important to find a way to get comfortable with risk if you believe in your purpose and you have a plan.
2. If you are risk-averse, taking the time to establish a safety net—whether it's a hiring strategy, financial plan, or something else—to mitigate risk-related fears can make all the difference in achieving your goals.

Jennifer Ferrari's Story: Leading a Team Through Change

No one—and we mean *no one*—predicted the chaos that ensued in 2020. Not a single sector was exempt from the seismic shifts in our society's habits and ways of working. However, out of all the sectors, education was hit particularly hard as students packed up their things and turned their kitchen tables into classrooms. Jennifer Ferrari, the CEO of the Education Research and Development Institute (ERDI), found herself and the company she led at the center of this chaotic storm. Though her team prefers structure, Jennifer's empathetic leadership style and clear vision for the organization allowed them to successfully navigate the changing circumstances together.

ERDI is a 35-year-old research and development organization that convenes executive school district and company leaders to collaboratively shape and influence the products and services that support PK–12 education. Framed around the most current problems in education, district leaders provide education companies with a critical feedback loop to better understand school district needs, and education companies use that information to improve their products. During normal times, this process flowed. In 2020, everything changed. The transition to remote learning increased the influx of problems and introduced an entirely new set of challenges alongside of them. ERDI's work doubled in complexity. Reflecting on the early days of the pandemic, Jennifer said, "It was impossible to keep up. We were responding in real time to so many different challenges as they presented themselves. The entire field of education was exhausted. There was no playbook. There were no structures and systems. Everything felt new."

Jennifer and her team were up for the task. ERDI's team members reflect the empathy, passion, and calculated risk-taking needed to achieve the organization's mission. As a leader, Jennifer loves the challenge of creating systems in collaboration with a team that is empowered to make decisions. They knew they needed to work together to manage the constantly evolving panorama of education during

2020 and 2021. At first, the constant changes in policy on a national and state level nearly pushed Jen and her team over the edge. In this context, her love of creating new systems and building culture would face its greatest challenge yet. When a leader commits to a mission, her employees count on her to deliver. This new and unknown context created an external InhibitHER that directly challenged their mission. While Jennifer was eager to address the challenges that the education space was facing, her team depended on the structure and reassurance of the process. So how, as a leader, did she manage a group who thrived on structure during a time of chaos and unpredictability?

First: empathy. "The team needed more caretaking and reassurance this year. Additionally, it goes without saying, everything felt extra risky because we were in no-man's-land. So many companies were struggling to just *make it*, so the inclination toward willing risk acceptance was lower than typical. I'm hopeful that we will learn from the experience of moving education online in 2020 due to the pandemic that we can afford to take greater risks in the future." With a lower risk tolerance and a higher need for full disclosure, her team needed her additional support. Jennifer chose to meet her team with empathy, listen to their concerns, and double down on finding solutions and systems so they could continue to provide much-needed guidance and leadership to both their school district and education company leaders.

Entrepreneurial skills and traits emerge in times of flux when adaptation is key to survival. Jennifer knew she needed to dig deep, charge ahead, and build a culture of confidence and creative problem-solving to survive the COVID-19 crisis. Now more than ever, due to an ever-changing landscape, she needed to be more methodical in her approach to address the unprecedented challenges facing the K–12 sector. Her first ActivateHER was empathy, but it wasn't the only one she leveraged. Her second step was to provide a nurturing space for problem-solving and design thinking. No question would be discounted. No idea would be dismissed. Across all projects, Jennifer and her team strategized ways to adapt the business to the pandemic.

To facilitate de-risked ideation and innovation, Jennifer had to establish a culture of trust. Her team needed to know that she trusted them to make decisions without constant oversight or approval. Equally important was the understanding that they knew she valued their experience and loyalty. To ensure the team wouldn't feel micromanaged, she made workflow changes, like giving feedback on a project after completion instead of consistently throughout its creation. She focused on setting crystal clear and measurable goals and then inspired her team to work freely within the guideposts of the process. Having served at every level in public education—classroom teacher, assistant principal, principal, assistant superintendent, and chief school officer—she understood how important it was to communicate with stakeholders and keep those connections open. When she shared the vision for the organization with her team, it was a top priority to make sure that they stayed connected to their shared purpose and allowed their "why" to be the lighthouse in the tempest.

These leadership changes helped Jennifer's team navigate the pandemic and not only achieve their full potential but also grow the organization during this unpredictable time. They also helped ERDI to innovate new thought leadership and research programs through an incredibly destabilizing time in education. From her story on how she carefully navigated the crisis, we learn the following lessons:

1. Teams that prefer structure can struggle to adapt in chaotic times.
2. Managing structure amid chaos is achievable if the leader breaks down goals into manageable steps, demonstrates trust in the work of the team, and successfully connects them to their greater purpose.

Weaving together the stories of women who have overcome external InhibitHERs illuminated just how many obstacles women must overcome to rise to the top. Even though all of the InnovateHERs we interviewed are currently in leadership positions, for some, it was a longer and more arduous path. While these InhibitHERs are out of their control, the InnovateHERs' responses to these challenges shaped them as professionals. They developed remarkable skills and communities of support as they employed their entrepreneurial mindset to navigate the tricky waters of building a career. Across the board, we were surprised and moved at the grace and eloquence with which the women described how, despite adversity, they yet managed to build careers defined by purpose and authentic to their life experiences.

CHAPTER 9

The Main ActivateHER–Mentorship

It may surprise you to learn that not one single InnovateHER got to where she is today without the continuous help of mentors throughout her career. Of all the ActivateHERs we have addressed, mentorship is the thread that weaves through all the stories of success and stands as the golden standard for how to scale the ranks at a purpose-driven (and really any) organization.

No matter how entrepreneurial, how innovative, or how persistent the woman, every single InnovateHER we interviewed attributed a part of her success to good mentorship. In some cases, this mentorship presented itself as intentional—the kind that is mutually agreed upon—but in others, it occurred by virtue of observation, sometimes even manifesting in the form of observing a parent, grandparent, sibling, or friend. Regardless of how it showed up in the lives of our InnovateHERs, mentorship was ubiquitous in every story, across the board.

What makes a mentor? Joysy John said it best when she defined great mentors as "people who open doors, who listen, who share their journeys, and who guide you to find your own answers to your personal and professional dilemmas." For many of our InnovateHERs, mentors also provided important encouragement to help them strive for the things they wanted.

When Krishanti O'Mara Vignarajah discussed her White House experience, she said, "My mantra was 'you have to see it to be it' because I do think it is incredibly important for people to see women who look like you going for things in a big way. When you see them serving in certain roles, it's just exciting. For me, seeing a powerful and petite woman senator hailing from the great state of Maryland was a real booster and was a real influencer in my decision to run for office."

While mentors come in different shapes and sizes, the one thing they have in common is the ability to play the important role of influencer and guide. Our InnovateHERs provided eight key takeaways about the role that mentors play:

1. **Positive, women role models at home are often the first mentors in an InnovateHER's life.**

   Lezli Baskerville: "My mother was my mentor. I had the highest respect for her. And she was the most generous, caring person that I've met in my life. She was optimistic. I knew that she was doing great things, but at her funeral, I realized that she put 17 members of her faculty through PhD programs. So that's the type of person she was."

2. **What happens at home can provide clarity about the goals we need to set for ourselves.**

   Monica Valrani: "My parents sent me to the best schools possible, but they were never too concerned about my grades. I think maybe that's why I never really pushed myself to study further. I didn't think it was important—but I regret that now. Which is why when it comes to my children, my boys often joke with me, 'Mom, you're like a tiger mom!' But for me, a good education is a non-negotiable, and I wanted my children to have that from the start."

3. **Simply setting an example can be the most powerful form of mentorship.**

Margaret Huber: "*I look to successful leaders. I tried to model some of my approaches and behaviors on what they were doing. For example, I've benefited from working for some outstanding ambassadors, who I admired greatly, who lead by example.*"

4. **The first place to begin looking for mentors is in your workplace. Oftentimes these mentors become important lifelong allies throughout your career.**

Lisa Schmucki: "*While working on a research project for Time-Life Books, I met Myril Axelrod, who was VP of qualitative research at Young and Rubicam. She was a brilliant, intuitive research and writer, and I was blessed to have her as a lifelong mentor and friend from the moment we met. She was magical in her ability to talk with consumers and get them to reveal what was really important to them and what their inner desires were and relate that to marketing and product development. She always made me feel smart and capable, and her advice taught me how to be a better, more customer-centric entrepreneur.*"

5. **People who have been mentored pay it forward by serving as a mentor to others.**

Maia Sharpley: "*I've had great mentors around me, both men and women, who have helped me and set a good example, and I always try to do the same—it's important to pay it forward. Because I've been helped, I turn around and help someone up and am thrilled to see them succeed. One of my mentees, who I have been working with for several years, and I recently met for dinner where she was brimming with excitement as she shared, 'Maia! I have to let you know that I just made partner! It's not public yet, but...' For me, it's so rewarding to watch young women go after their dreams and make their dreams a reality."*

6. **It's good to have formal mentorship, but you can also just begin by getting advice when you feel stuck.**

Patricia Scanlon: "There's often no one right answer, and being an entrepreneur means not being afraid of trial and error, of learning on the journey. When making a strategic or important tactical decision, I try to start by being open-minded. I reach out and talk to people who've walked in my shoes before with a similar challenge or decision to make. I listen to what they're saying, digest it whole, and then, I go away and listen to myself, decide on a path, and move decisively forward."

7. **Because there are fewer women leaders, it may be easier to get men to become mentors. The gender of your mentor doesn't matter, but it is important to have someone who believes in you and your career trajectory.**

Sherrie Westin: "When I held positions in my early career in Washington, people would often ask who had been my female mentors. I had amazing mentors—but they were all men! I had many women to admire from afar, but none were my bosses or mentors in the workplace. One of the leaders I most admired was Tom Murphy, CEO of Cap Cities/ABC, who empowered us to take responsibility, make decisions, and not be afraid to take risks. He always said it was okay to make mistakes—as long as they were honest and that you learned from them."

8. **Woman-to-woman mentorship is especially helpful when making work-life balance decisions.**

> **Lisa Hall**: *"I was chief of staff for my mentor. She was extraordinary. In those early days, when I was working for her, it was the example that she set of balancing family—prioritizing—she was really skilled at being in the moment. I would see her shift from something like having a parent-teacher conversation to a discussion on legal affairs without missing a beat. She modeled how to prioritize what was in front of her and not be distracted."*

On the path to becoming an InnovateHER, you undoubtedly will need mentorship along the way. In this chapter, Kathy shares her story about how both a mentee and a mentor helped her to become a transformative leader of impactful initiatives. She shares why she became a mentor and provides tips and advice for securing a great mentor to guide you on your path to the top.

The Importance of Mentors

Kathy Hurley's Story: Why You Need One and Why You Should Become One

Forty years of experience as an executive in the education industry has taught me a thing or two about the importance of good mentorship. My training to become a mentor and a mentee began long before I entered the professional world. My first unofficial mentor role was to my three younger siblings. At a young age, I was a sponge for learning from others and was always seeking out good role models to emulate. I wanted to learn from them, and I wanted to share what I had learned with others—siblings, friends, and even strangers. In high school, I was involved in student leadership and various clubs—I was even captain of the cheerleading team. My senior year, the description under my yearbook picture reads, "Her enthusiasm knows no bounds." I've tried to carry that enthusiasm and love of working with people throughout my career. That enthusiasm carried over to college, where

I realized that the one thing I wanted to do most of all was make a difference by helping others.

Therefore, it's no surprise that my first job in the "real world" was as a special education teacher in New Jersey. Nothing could have prepared me for the role of mentor more than being a special education teacher. Teacher, advisor, guide, counselor, tutor, instructor, coach—every synonym for mentoring was used daily as I worked with special needs students. While I played the role of mentor, I learned that there was much, much more to being a good mentor than guiding or instructing someone. Working with special needs students taught me the intangible skills of empathy, compassion, patience, servanthood, and generosity—qualities also found in good mentors. More importantly, I discovered that I needed mentors and actively sought out veteran teachers and administrators to guide me in my new profession.

Unlikely Mentors

"Search for role models you can look up to and people who take an interest in your career. But here's an important warning: You don't have to have mentors who look like you. Had I been waiting for a Black, female Soviet specialist mentor, I would still be waiting. Most of my mentors have been old White men, because they were the ones who dominated my field."

—*Condoleeza Rice,*
Former U.S. Secretary of State

When I made the decision to leave the classroom to join the private-sector side of education, I took that wealth of knowledge with me to the corporate world. I quickly learned that the corporate side of the education industry was very different from the public side. Forty years ago, the private-sector side of education was dominated by men. Like Condoleeza Rice, if I had waited for someone who looked like me, I would've waited a long time. For me, the role models available were the men leading the industry. Fortunately, I had several top-level executives who took an interest in my career. Not only did they see my potential, but they also actively helped me network and develop the skills necessary to move up the ladder.

On the private side of the education sector, I have taken the "entrepreneurial leap" by moving from large education publishing firms and EdTech companies to small startups. Once the startups were self-sustaining, I would move again to another challenge—maybe a mid-level company trying to break into the larger ranks or a large company trying to get its hands around a recent acquisition. In each move, I always looked for a mentor or sought the guidance of a mentor to help me navigate the changes ahead. Looking back on my career, I realize now that one of my best mentors was my late husband, Charles Blaschke. I met him about the time that I started at IBM, which was one of my first jobs with a big, public company. I was an executive in their K–12 division. Charles had his own company, Education TURNKEY Solutions, which helped education companies under federal and state education policy and directed the dollars that flowed to policy priorities. He helped me understand the nuances of policy and how federal and state dollars impacted decision-making by superintendents and top-level administrators. Having him as a mentor while I was at IBM really helped me grow professionally.

Fortunately for me, IBM also had a great purpose-driven employee culture. They were committed to developing the individual because they wanted all employees to reach their full potential. I had one manager there who really impacted me in a big way. After receiving my employee evaluation, which admittedly was a mixed review, my manager said, "Don't worry about the low scores because I am going to help you become the number one employee in our division!" From that moment on, he transformed from a manager to a mentor. Most managers don't do that. A good mentor will tell you what to improve and actively work to help you become better at what you do. That is the difference between a mentor and manager.

While I needed mentors that were in my profession, the more I progressed in my career, I found myself gravitating to mentors who were not in the same sector but who were leaders in their sector. Through my networking and involvement on boards and philanthropic organizations, I discovered other successful professionals who had a wealth of experience to share. I developed relationships with these people and built a cross-industry network of people who helped me build the skills necessary to be successful across industry lines. Since many of the boards I served on were in education, I often found myself serving as a mentor to other board members who needed the expertise of someone from within our sector.

Women and the Time Commitment Quandary

"My mother was my mentor. She had me when she was 42. She got her PhD when she 62. She was a maverick. You know, she came from a culture where you were supposed to be married a decade before she got married. She came to the US on her own, before my grandmother kind of pulled her back and said, 'If you're going to try to go abroad, you better be married beforehand.' So, her strategy was there were some things that she bided by and other things that she bucked. I think that was a very important life lesson for me—to do things on my own."

—Krishanti O'Mara Vignarajah, CEO,
Lutheran Immigration and Refugee Service

I have observed a fascinating theme throughout my career about how women and men approach mentorship opportunities. An example that I like to share with people is from a personal experience I had when I retired from Pearson. Before I retired, I was asked to give remarks to a group of sales representatives. There were about two hundred reps in attendance—about half men, half women. At the end of my remarks, I said, "If I can be of help to any of you in reaching out to school districts or making industry connections or just be a voice of experience, please find me at the end of today's meeting, and I'll be happy to give you my information so we can stay in touch." I had five people take me up on my offer of assistance—and they were all men. I was disappointed that none of the women in the room approached me at the end, but I understood why—*time*.

Women, by nature, are multi-taskers—we're working, running households, volunteering, and so forth. We must prioritize our commitments, and all too often, we eliminate mentorship and networking opportunities because they take time, and time is our most precious commodity. However, making the time is worth it, and it pays off in the end! Jennifer Ferrari does it well: In the car, she commits to making at least three phone calls a week to women she either mentors or is being mentored by to check in and see how they are doing. As demonstrated by the stories shared in this book, women with an entrepreneurial mindset embrace mentorship opportunities. (And, not surprisingly, many of the women in this book said their mothers were their first mentors.) Their stories illuminate the importance of searching for mentors, building relationships, and then paying it forward by mentoring other women who can benefit from their guidance.

One observation that I made early in my career was that men made time to network and to develop mentor–mentee relationships. Men are great at taking advantage of those relationships. The cliché "good ol' boys' network" is a cliché for a reason—it's true. Entrepreneurial, driven, ambitious women do not need to blaze the trail alone. It is imperative that we leverage the experience of people who have gone before us—purpose-driven women, and men, who can shine the light of experience on our trail.

Women Helping Women

"I think women are expected to behave very differently than male entrepreneurs. In my case, it has helped to

have strong women surrounding me on my entrepreneurial journey. My grandmother was my biggest advocate when I was growing up—she was the principal of the school I graduated from, and she taught me how to advocate for myself, speak in public, and be fearless."

—Ana Hidalgo, CEO, founder of LAB XXI and ReinventED Schools

In the 1980s, the education publishing industry was changing with the advent of personal computers and the incorporation of computer labs in K–12 schools. Many of the entrepreneurs leading the way were men, but there were a growing number of women joining the ranks of the EdTech world. It was then that I had the good fortune of meeting Ellen Bialo, a true trailblazer and someone a mentor for me. Ellen understood the importance of networking to help women develop mentor–mentee relationships. So, after a few meetings (which may have included a couple of cocktails), Ellen and I, along with a small group of women executives, started an informal group called the DOLS (Dirty Old Ladies of Software). We organized dinners and modest receptions at education industry trade shows and events around the country. Initially, we had 20 to 30 women attend these events. The gatherings proved an excellent way to meet new people in the industry, develop impactful, meaningful relationships, and learn from each other. Today, the DOLS has more than 800 members, and we still gather at education industry events—only now we also host regional events to give women in our industry the opportunity to get together more often. Through this one network, I've made lifelong friends, and I've been able to serve as a mentor to younger women in the industry.

While the DOLS provided one avenue to create networking and mentorship opportunities, I created other ways to recognize and promote women in the nascent education technology sector. While men were driving the private side of the education technology world, women in the classroom were the ones implementing the technology. To recognize these women, I and my industry colleagues Deb deVries and Pat Walkington started the Making IT Happen program to recognize educators who were making information technology happen in the classroom. In the beginning, the recipients were women. We hosted Making IT Happen award ceremonies at education conferences around the country. Not only did these events promote and recognize women, but they also provided opportunities to meet other successful women in our field and learn about their journeys. In the beginning, the award was given to women, but as time passed, we found "a few good men" to recognize with the award. Today, Making IT Happen is an award program run by the International Society for Technology in Education and is given to educators all over the world!

Certain other great organizations are also dedicated to creating networking and mentorship opportunities in the education and purpose-driven sectors:

- The ASU-GSV Women's Network is perfect for women entrepreneurs in the EdTech space.
- The Women Administrator's Education PowerTrip, founded by Marilyn Schutz, is an event that takes place every summer and is designed to specifically help women leaders in the education space network and learn from one another.
- The American Association of School Administrator's Women in School Leadership Initiative is designed to give women a voice while sharing initiatives and successes with each other.
- Athena Alliance is an executive community that makes it easy and accessible for women leaders to learn from their peers.

These are just a few examples of the many groups that have been created to help women connect with and learn from one another. Learning to engage and support other women is the linchpin to ensuring that women not only meet their potential but also move into important leadership roles.

Women Recognizing Other Women

Throughout my career, I've tried to make a point of recognizing other women in my field who have significant achievements and who are making a difference. Like the women we recognized with the Making IT Happen award, it was equally important for me to nominate colleagues for prestigious industry sector awards. Not only can we serve as mentors for one another, but we can also lift one another up to make sure women are visible as top performers in our field. As someone fortunate enough to receive the Association of Educational Publishers Hall of Fame Award and the Software Information & Industry Association EdTech Lifetime Achievement award, I have felt that I need to pay it forward by nominating top-performing women colleagues for these and other prestigious industry-recognized awards. We can celebrate our successes with each other, but how much more impactful is it to ensure our successes are seen by everyone in our chosen field?

Mentors Make Time

> *"I think part of the responsibility of a leader is to pay it forward. If you think about the people that influenced your life—whether it was teachers or the mentors I've had—I found time. I very actively reach into [my] organization. It's my responsibility to do that. I have to carve out time—it's important. I think part of mentoring others is also making yourself better. It is the same reason I sit on boards. It makes me a better CEO if I'm on the other side of the table too."*
>
> *—Jamie Candee, CEO, Edmentum*

Although most of my mentors were men when I moved from the classroom to the education publishing sector, that changed when I was hired by Pearson to serve as Senior Vice President of strategic partnerships. At the time, Pearson was led by Marjorie Scardino, who had assumed leadership in 1997, so becoming the first woman to lead an FTSE 100 company. I believe it also made her the first woman to lead a major educational publishing house. When she became CEO, Pearson was a disparate conglomeration of companies ranging from Madame Tussaud's (of waxed celebrity fame) to the Lazard investment firm to the Financial Times of London to Penguin Publishing. After selling off some of the less profitable businesses, Marjorie reorganized the company into three divisions: financial publishing, consumer publishing, and education publishing. It became Pearson Education. She bet big on education, and by the time I joined Pearson in 2004, it had become the largest education company in the world! Marjorie had gained widespread renown.

Pearson is a London-based company. When I joined, I was based out of their New York office. It never crossed my mind at the time that I would engage with Marjorie, much less have her become one of my most impactful mentors. However, as my role with the company grew, I traveled quite a bit to London, and she would come to New York for meetings. I observed how Marjorie interacted with others. Unlike other CEOs, she had little to no ego. Whether she was interacting with a customer, another executive, or a student in a school, she was always gracious and appreciative. Her interactions were sincere because she focused all her attention on the person or people in the moment. No job was ever too small, yet she never shied away from the big decisions or challenges.

A piece of advice that she shared with me—and with everyone at Pearson—was to "err on the side of generosity." We all need a little grace extended to us when we make mistakes or need encouragement. Now more than ever, the world needs people to err on the side of generosity in time, words, and actions.

For any CEO, time is a precious asset. What set Marjorie apart was her ability to *make time* for others. She took the time to get to know me, engage with me, and help me navigate my career. After retiring from Pearson, I still reach out to her for advice and guidance—and she remains gracious with her time and wisdom.

Qualities of a Good Mentor

Marjorie embodied all the qualities of a good mentor. One might ask: How do you know what qualities to look for in a mentor–mentee relationship? Finding a good mentor is like people watching—except, instead of just watching, you identify qualities you are looking to develop and find the people who display those qualities.

Identify people who are especially good at their craft. Study how they do the following:

- Behave and carry themselves
- Interact with others
- Address conflict
- Celebrate successes
- Evaluate failures

Search for someone empathetic, confident, and genuinely interested in others, not only a good listener but also trustworthy. Does this person have the availability to mentor you, and are they someone who will be honest and frank with you? Learning hard truths is just as important as hearing words of encouragement. The very best mentors build legacies by passing their knowledge and experience to the next generation.

Mentors Are Everywhere

"If I hadn't had mentors, I wouldn't be here today. I'm a product of great mentoring, great coaching…Coaches or mentors are very important. They could be anyone— your husband, other family members, or your boss."

—*Indra Nooyi, Former Chair of the*
Board and CEO of PepsiCo

Mentor–mentee relationships are not limited to the workplace. Boards, associations, business organizations (chambers, rotaries, etc.), volunteer organizations, and places of worship are all excellent avenues by which get involved and find people with diverse backgrounds, including ages, races, genders, who can help create a diversity of thought and experiences.

After my time at Pearson, I spent a year at Harvard's Advanced Leadership Initiative (ALI), where I met a wonderfully diverse group of people from around the world who were focused on serving others after retiring from amazing careers. Some of the women featured in this book attended the ALI and have become good friends and mentors to me.

Many of my colleagues at ALI were transitioning from important leadership roles to the next phases of their careers, which entailed giving back to the community at large as well as finding young people to mentor. Watching this group of well-accomplished people interact with their younger counterparts at Harvard was inspirational. I know that many of the relationships formed during that time are remain strong and that many of these people continue to serve as mentors years later.

After completing the ALI program, I and my good friend and longtime industry colleague Deb deVries co-founded Girls Thinking Global, a nonprofit dedicated to helping organizations that help adolescent girls and young women to connect with each other to leverage resources and to learn from each other. During this time, I met Zoë Timms, featured in this book. Zoë is the Executive Director of the Women's Education Project, which partners with girl- and women-focused NGOs to extend its Leadership Academy, which helps young women ages 15–24 to build confidence and explore their interests and career opportunities while also acquiring the job-ready skills necessary to gain employment. The Leadership Academy explicitly incorporates a supportive community of peers, mentors, and role models. The Women's Education Project supports NGOs in India and Bangladesh and is having a tremendous impact—and the mentorship aspect of the program is a pivotal reason for its success. Many of these young women have never had the good fortune of having a mentor guide them on a leadership path. Having this type of support and encouragement keeps them engaged and connected.

At that time, I also partnered with my sister in law, Priscilla Shumway, to write my first book, *Real Women, Real Leaders: Surviving and Succeeding in the Business World*. The book shared the stories of 24 women leaders who utilized key competencies that Harvard researchers identified as crucial to leadership excellence. The stories those women shared and the competencies that they nurtured had a common theme: the importance of mentors in the development of their key competencies and improvement in their areas of weakness.

Rising Tides Lift All Boats

In the end, mentorship relationships are about lifting each other up. Through intentional, dedicated relationships, our successes reverberate, and the adage about rising tides lifting all boats becomes true. If we dig deeper into all the stories of successful entrepreneurs, we usually find a mentor—a parent, teacher, friend, colleague—who not only encouraged them but also modeled success for them.

As demonstrated by the stories shared throughout this book, women with an entrepreneurial mindset have been mentees and have become mentors as they have progressed in their careers. Those who have become mentors agree that they learn as much from mentoring others as they did from their own mentors.

Recently, Lisa Schmucki (also featured in this book) surveyed women administrators from the Women's Fellowship Breakfast at a meeting of the Education Research and Development Institute. During the breakfast, she asked the women to write down what most helped them professionally, personally, and emotionally. They mentioned the following common themes and activities:

- Mentoring
- Networking

- Collaborating with innovative colleagues
- Working remotely yet staying connected
- Reaching out to others

While there were others on the list, I thought these selections were highly informative because they demonstrate the need for connection, interaction, and collaboration. Our desire to learn from and support each other is strong, and when we do this in a productive, deliberate way, we all benefit. Even though I retired from Pearson, I remain active in the education industry as well as with various women's organizations, such as the Women's Education Project. Whether I am consulting for a private company or serving as a director on a nonprofit board, I continue to serve as a mentor to women *and* men seeking to further their careers or grow their organizations.

In closing, I will leave you with the words of the inimitable poet, memoirist, and civil rights activist, Maya Angelou:

> *"In order to be a mentor, and an effective one, one must care. You must care. You don't have to know how many square miles are in Idaho. You don't need to know what is the chemical makeup or the chemistry of blood or water. Know what you know and care about the person, care about what you know and care about the person you're sharing with."*

CHAPTER 10

Rise to the Top

When we—Bobbi and Kathy—dreamt up this book, we had no idea where it would take us. Maybe we would just collect the experiences of the women we encountered throughout our careers. Or maybe we would write and publish a more research-driven book to investigate the connection between purpose-driven work and the entrepreneurial mindset based on the initial research on educational leaders. Regardless of what we imagined, we have both been amazed and awed by the women in our lives—our colleagues and friends— who have inspired us with such fascinating, stirring, poignant, and at times heartbreaking stories behind their success in the purpose-driven, social-impact space. We never thought that each story would hold such deep connections between purpose, identity, and skills built along the way to the top. The gift we have been given through writing *InnovateHERs* is an intimate look at the long, arduous but incredibly rewarding and engaging process of building a person who does remarkable things for the world.

An InnovateHER is an entrepreneurial woman who leverages her traits and skills to create a positive impact in the world and achieve a greater personal purpose. She is brave, she is bold and innovative, and she has both triumphed and failed along the way to success. This collection of stories takes us through the journey of *how* that purpose is defined, *what* entrepreneurial mindset traits and skills helped along the way, and *why* it is so important to these women to make a difference in the world. Finally, and most importantly, these stories no longer live in the minds of our InnovateHERs but have now been documented and shared so that you—and other future InnovateHERs—can learn how to rise to the top too.

Today, when we hear the stories of successful women, we tend to get the "finished" version. Maybe she is featured in a *Forbes* article, speaking at a conference, posting an impressive accomplishment on LinkedIn, or being interviewed on a podcast. What we see is who she is after years and years of working her way to the top. The gift this book gives is the opportunity to start a dialogue and ask, "*How* did you get so polished? Which key traits and skills can help *you* rise to the top?" By looking at a group of fascinating women who approach their work in a very different light than men—and quite honestly, one another—we can see how they became successful in their own rights.

There Is Still Work to Be Done

Our research shows that women approach innovation using different skills and traits than men do. For example, women may struggle more with self-confidence, lack of funding, and financial insecurities, and they may naturally prefer more structure, but they shine in their passion, empathy, and persistence. Whereas entrepreneurial men tend to be more focused on the future and prefer to work independently, women are focused on building the here and now. They want to be impactful, but they understand the importance of building the safety nets that will catch risk-takers when they fall. They know relationships will sustain an organization through challenging times and that passion will keep an organization's mission focused on purpose through challenging times.

This is the Portrait of an InnovateHER.

With more than 1 billion jobs positioned to be eliminated due to technology, explosive population growth in developing countries, and unprecedented challenges to our global infrastructure, it's never been more important to promote leaders who think and approach the world differently. We desperately need innovation across all the purpose-driven sectors, and we need the brightest, most diverse entrepreneurial teams on deck to tackle these challenges. Purpose-driven industries that include sectors like healthcare, environment, education, and nongovernmental organizations are rapidly gaining attention. The global education market alone is on track to be at least a $10 trillion dollar industry by 2030,[29] and healthcare has already surpassed that and is well into the trillions almost a decade before education.[30] As these conditions unfold, and with most startups fighting for a slice of the overcrowded real estate or energy markets, a select group of entrepreneurs has been trailblazing a path to define a better world. Their unconventional leadership, combined with an accelerated pace of change on a global scale, means getting the right people into leadership positions could have a massive impact.

The Takeaways for Future InnovateHERs

With the InnovateHERs' stories behind us, we are left with the lessons collected from 27 remarkable women (29, counting ourselves) who are achieving remarkable things. As we download the tapestry of so many diverse careers and pathways, it's impossible to ignore what they have in common. Though no two paths were the same, certain lessons span the stories of InnovateHERs.

Wherever you might currently be in your career and wherever you might want to go, keep in mind the key guideposts:

1. You already have unique entrepreneurial traits. Identify them.
2. You can build entrepreneurial skills. Work to strengthen them.
3. It doesn't just depend on you. Examine and understand your internal and external InhibitHERs.
4. You can turn your barriers into assets. Convert InhibitHERs into ActivateHERs.

5. Mentors, mentors, mentors. Pull in others and build community along your journey to success.

6. Let your purpose guide your path. Keep aiming for that north star.

7. Have fun—enjoy your work—and if you are doing it right, the line between work and play blurs!

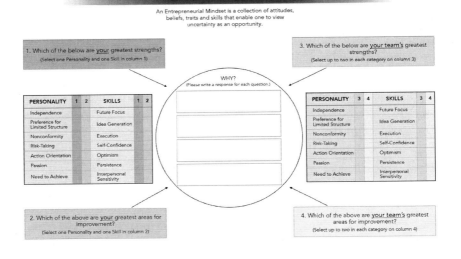

The Generation in Waiting

What we have learned from the women interviewed for this book exceeds all our wildest expectations. Oftentimes, we sat after interviews mulling over the deeply personal stories we had just heard and repeated to one another, "What an *incredible* woman! I had no idea all she had to overcome to get to where she is today." It became so clear that behind each InnovateHER's success is a story of hard work, resilience, sacrifice, and tough decisions well beyond the workplace. Each woman is a collage of experiences that have helped her build the entrepreneurial mindset to inform her decisions and continuously help her crystalize her vision.

Throughout this process, we defined why this book was so important for us to write. Building an InnovateHER is the work of a lifetime. It is a long, messy process with lots of ups and downs along the way. By collecting stories, we can pass on knowledge to the next generation of InnovateHERs. This, above all else, is a crucial part of our mission. Oftentimes, the women we interviewed began recounting their journey to success from as far back as childhood. Maybe it began with an experience that shaped their pathways, an important family member whom they admired, or a set of values instilled in them at a young age. As we look at the current and next generation of girls, we should see them as future InnovateHERs and help to develop their entrepreneurial skills as soon as possible.

Perhaps these future InnovateHERs include your daughter, granddaughter, niece, or younger sister. She could be the student day-dreaming in your class, the assistant looking to scale the ranks, or the young idealist setting the stage to start her own organization. These women-in-waiting are the next in line to receive the baton and become strong, unique leaders in the purpose-driven space. As in many of the stories we heard, their traits, skills, and purpose are being defined as we speak. Most importantly, you can have more influence on them than you know.

So, take a deep breath, walk to the nearest mirror, see yourself for a long moment, and ask, "How can I become or help develop the next InnovateHER?"

Speaking of YOU

Do you consider yourself an InnovateHER? What entrepreneurial traits and skills do you have that make you uniquely positioned to make a difference? When you were reading these stories, did you nod along with the lived experiences? Do you dream of achieving purpose and rising to the top of your field? Are you ready to embrace the journey to leadership?

If so, *InnovateHERs* is the start of a long journey for you. Perhaps you already possess the need to achieve, passion, calculated risk-taking, and action orientation, and now, you are interested in honing those skills or building new ones. Perhaps you are like some of our InnovateHERs, and you struggle with self-confidence, persistence, idea generation and execution, or optimism. These stories are designed to share women's words of wisdom and real-life examples of how to apply what they did—and how they did it—to your life.

We wish you all the best as you find your path and rise to the top.

ACKNOWLEDGEMENTS

This book has been in the making for many years, as we have both explored our entrepreneurial mindsets, our leadership styles, and our personal journeys to success. Along the way, we have had many mentors and role models. They have been both men and women. They have been both older and younger. They live around the world and close to home. But most of all, they were wonderful mentors who became, and remain, good friends.

First, we want to thank our families.

(Bobbi) To my mother, who was my first role model, friend, and loving parent who showed me how to be a great parent while having a career. To my father, who was my biggest fan. To my children, Debra and Jonathan (and their spouses), my enthusiastic cheerleaders who have shown me how to learn and how to make a difference. They are always there when I need them and let me be a big part of their lives and their families, especially with my grandsons, Joseph and Robert.

(Kathy) To my siblings, Jack, Lucy, and Peggy, my sister-in-law Priscilla, and my nieces and nephews who are always supportive and bring such joy to my life. To my late parents, John and Lucille Hurley, who gave us an ideal, loving childhood and encouraged us to pursue our dreams. They would be so happy to know that we have stayed so close as a family. A big thank you to my late husband, Charles Blaschke, who always said I could do most anything I put in my mind to do. He was also my mentor, friend, and the smartest person I knew, and he will always be a big part of my life.

To our most amazing group of friends—Linda Roberts, Sue Talley, Susan Harman, Marge Cappo, Karen Billings, Deb deVries, and Jenny House—who have been amazing InnovateHERs with purpose-driven missions. We have been friends and colleagues for many years and have been there for each other through many life cycles—celebrations, heartbreaks, recognitions, and remembrances.

A special shout out to those who have helped us rise to the top.

(Bobbi) To those in the industry that became my friends, teachers, mentors, bosses, and partners: Susan Harman, who taught me the difference between investment banking and commercial banking; John Grillos, who told me he would teach me everything about investment banking if I taught him everything about education and technology; Granetta Blevins, who was always there to make sure my crazy ideas were financially sound; Tom Sherman, my doctoral advisor, who believed in my vision that computers would change education; and Jack Lynch, who taught me how to take my innovative ideas and build a strategy to make them happen.

(Bobbi) To the coauthors and co-creators of my articles, books, and educational software products and the mentors who helped me create and innovate: Leslie Mitts, Alan November, David Weinman, Jenny Zapf, Serrano LeGrand, Rachel Ebby, Cat McManus, Deneen Frazier-Bowen, Cheryl Weiner, Anita Kopec, Kate Walker, Betsy Corcoran, and to the many others not mentioned by name, through EDSi, the Milken-PennGSE Business Plan Competition, and other incubators and competitions. A special thanks to Scott McNealy for choosing me to create and run Curriki, an open educational resources platform that made content free and open to educators around the world.

(Kathy) To Tom Greaves, Mark Nieker, Deb deVries, Kathy Kleibacker, Deb Delisle, Gary Mainor, Eric Robertson, Chuck Amos, Evan St. Lifer and Liz Ralston and my fabulous ladies film festival group who have been my go-to people over the years. To my good friend Berj Akian, CEO of ClassLink, who has generously supported this book project as well as my first publication. I have learned so much from each of them, and they have added magic and laughter to my life. A very special thank you to Ginny Kirkland and Mary McGoldrick, who have both worked with me for 20-plus years and who were critical to my success over the years. Finally, I want to thank my many friends and colleagues from the education technology and publishing industry who have traveled with me on this amazing journey over the last fifty years. The generosity and support of this tight-knit community is like no other and as a group, they have been critical to my personal and professional growth and success.

We also want to thank the students, the mentees, and the many entrepreneurs we have had the privilege to work with, mentor, and invest in their dreams and ventures.

(Bobbi) I hope I was able to teach my students at Penn GSE, VA Tech, and Hollins College as much about how to think, to learn, and to innovate as they have taught me. Through EDSi, the Penn GSE incubator, I want to acknowledge the many entrepreneurs that were part of that community and who started and grew successful companies, or failed, learned, and tried again. These companies include Raise, Byndr, Mindprint Learning, Sophya (SoWork), RobotsLab, Fablevision, Mindstone, and many, many others.

We want to thank the reviewers for their support as well as our clients who have become dear friends and supporters. We want to acknowledge the people that made this book happen: our research partners at Penn GSE, Jenny and Serrano, and at the Eckerd College Center for Creative Leadership who developed the Entrepreneurial Mindset Profile®; our writing, marketing, and research team, Laura Smulian, Ginny Kirkland, and Bridget Foster; and the publishing team at Bublish, including Kathy Meis, Shilah LaCoe, and Nick Newton. Thank you to the team at ClassLink for your support and for providing us with a talented graphic artist, Cesar Marquez. Without each of you, this book would have never been completed. Thank you to everyone who researched, read, edited, and helped us get this book published.

There are so many other people to thank, and they know who they are. They have been there for our lifetime journey toward success. Our lives are filled with wonderful and loyal friends and mentors.

To all those who have changed and are changing education, learning, and purpose-driven endeavors, thank you. From those in startups to those in established companies and organizations and in purpose-driven endeavors, we thank you for the important work you are doing. You are our friends, mentors, and role models, but more importantly, you are making a difference in the world.

Finally, we want to thank each other for this special journey, the sharing of our stories, and our friendship.

> *Bobbi, I want to thank you for your passion and drive to get this book done.*

> *Kathy, I want to thank you for working so hard to share your experiences and network to identify and engage the right set of women role models and entrepreneurial thinkers for this book.*

—Bobbi Kurshan and Kathy Hurley

REFERENCES

[1] Global Workplace Analytics, & Lister, K. (2021, October 17). *Work-at-home after Covid-19 – Our forecast.* Global Workplace Analytics. https://globalworkplaceanalytics.com/work-at-home-after-covid-19-our-forecast

[2] Davis, M. H., Hall, J. A., & Mayer, P. S. (2016). Developing a new measure of entrepreneurial mindset: Reliability, validity, and implications for practitioners. *Consulting Psychology Journal: Practice and Research, 68*(1), 21–48. https://doi.org/10.1037/cpb0000045

[3] Schuyler, S., & Brennan, A. (2016). *Putting purpose to work: How to cultivate, communicate and sustain purpose at your organization.* PwC. https://www.pwc.com/us/en/about-us/corporate-responsibility/assets/pwc-putting-purpose-to-work-purpose-survey-report.pdf

[4] Lagerberg, F., & Schmidt, K. (2020). *Women in business 2020 report.* Grant Thornton International. https://www.grantthornton.global/globalassets/1.-member-firms/global/insights/women-in-business/2020/women-in-business-2020_report.pdf

[5] Wan, T. (2015, April 1). *Is education technology where women are starting to buck the tech world's sexist trends?* Fast Company. https://www.fastcompany.com/3043779/is-education-technology-where-women-are-starting-to-buck-the-tech-world

[6] Perry, M. J. (2020, October 15). *Women earned majority of doctoral degrees in 2019 for 11th straight year and outnumber men in grad school 141 to 100.* American Enterprise Institute - AEI. https://www.aei.org/carpe-diem/women-earned-majority-of-doctoral-degrees-in-2019-for-11th-straight-year-and-outnumber-men-in-grad-school-141-to-100/

[7] Dawson, J., Kersley, R., & Natella, S. (2016). *The CS Gender 3000: The reward for change.* Credit Suisse Research Institute. https://evolveetfs.com/wp-content/uploads/2017/08/Credit-Suisse-Reward-for-Change_1495660293279_2.pdf

[8] Abouzahr, K., Krentz, M., Harthorne, J., & Taplett, F. B. (2018, June 6). *Why women-owned startups are a better bet.* Boston Consulting Group. https://www.bcg.com/en-us/publications/2018/why-women-owned-startups-are-a-better-bet

[9] Mascarenhas, N. (2021, June 2). *Guild Education valued at $3.75 billion with newest round.* TechCrunch. https://techcrunch.com/2021/06/02/guild-education-valued-at-3-75-billion-with-newest-round/

[10] McGrath, M. (2021, September 16). *Spring Health notches a $190 million series C at a $2 billion valuation, making CEO April Koh the youngest woman to run a unicorn.* Forbes. https://www.forbes.com/sites/maggiemcgrath/2021/09/16/spring-health-notches-a-190-million-series-c-at-a-2-billion-valuation-making-ceo-april-koh-the-youngest-woman-to-run-a-unicorn/?sh=75ba127a4ced

[11] Alter, C. (2021, March 19). *How Whitney Wolfe herd turned a vision of a better internet into a billion-dollar brand.* Time. https://time.com/5947727/whitney-wolfe-herd-bumble/

[12] Scheidegger, J. (2019, October 3). *More women founders equals more women in executive roles.* Ewing Marion Kauffman Foundation. https://www.kauffman.org/currents/more-women-founders-more-women-executive-roles/

[13] Smith, C., Turner, S., Anderson, E., Atwell, J., Franklin, B., Haque, M., & Straus, J. (2016). *NVCA-Deloitte Human Capital Survey Report.* National Venture Capital Association. https://nvca.org/wp-content/uploads/2019/10/NVCA-Deloitte-Human-Capital-Survey-2016.pdf

[14] Catalyst. (2020, April 4). *Women in healthcare (quick take).* https://www.catalyst.org/research/women-in-healthcare/

[15] DeSilver, D. (2018, April 30). *Women scarce at top of U.S. business — and in the jobs that lead there.* Pew Research Center. https://www.

pewresearch.org/fact-tank/2018/04/30/women-scarce-at-top-of-u-s-business-and-in-the-jobs-that-lead-there/?utm_source=Pew%2BResearch%2BCenter&utm_campaign=7d1e5bf43c-EMAIL_CAMPAIGN_2018_05_15&utm_medium=email&utm_term=0_3e953b9b70-7d1e5bf43c-400316229

16 The Bureau for Employers' Activities (ACT/EMP). (2019). *Women in business and management: The business case for change.* International Labor Organization. https://www.ilo.org/wcmsp5/groups/public/---dgreports/---dcomm/---publ/documents/publication/wcms_700953.pdf

17 Imperative, & Tavis, A. (2015). *2015 Workforce Purpose Index.* Imperative. https://cdn.imperative.com/media/public/Purpose_Index_2015

18 Mercer. (2020). *Let's get real about equality: View key findings from the When Women Thrive 2020 Global Report.* https://www.mercer.com/content/dam/mercer/attachments/global/gl-2020-global-research-report-2020-highlights-flyer.pdf.

19 Rollings, M. (2018, October 1). *State of the workplace report: Gender.* Hive. https://hive.com/blog/state-of-workplace-gender/

20 Oxford University Press. (n.d.). Entrepreneur. In *Oxford learner's dictionary.* Retrieved September 08, 2021 from https://www.oxfordlearnersdictionaries.com/us/definition/english/entrepreneur

21 Edweb. (2019, June 13). *edWeb wins CODiE for best professional learning.* https://home.edweb.net/edweb-wins-codie-for-best-professional-learning/

22 Oxford University Press. (n.d.). Empathy. In *Oxford Learner's Dictionary.* Retrieved August 10, 2021 from https://www.oxfordlearnersdictionaries.com/us/definition/english/empathy

23 Ely, R. J., Stone, P., & Ammerman, C. (2014). *Rethink what you "know" about high-achieving women.* Harvard Business Review. Retrieved October 20, 2021 from https://hbr.org/2014/12/rethink-what-you-know-about-high-achieving-women

References

[24] University of Pennsylvania, Legrand, S., Zapf, J., & Kurshan, B. (2020). *Understanding the mindset of entrepreneurs working in P-20 education*. University of Pennsylvania.

[25] Cambridge University Press. (n.d.). Risk. In *Cambridge Dictionary*. Retrieved January 17, 2021 from https://dictionary.cambridge.org/us/dictionary/english/risk

[26] Financial Times. (2019, November 13). *Financial Times 100 BAME leaders influencing the tech sector: UK Black, Asian and minority ethnic individuals who are driving change.*

[27] Kim, J. Y., Kim, E., & Lee, I. (2021). Influence of self-esteem of middle school students for mental care on academic achievement: Based on the mediation effect of grit and academic enthusiasm. *International Journal of Environmental Research and Public Health*, *18*(13), Art. 7025. https://doi.org/10.3390/ijerph18137025

[28] Haselton, J. (2020, February 12). *Investing in women-led edtech startups is more than a matter of equity. it's also good business.* EdSurge. https://www.edsurge.com/news/2020-02-12-investing-in-women-led-edtech-startups-is-more-than-a-matter-of-equity-it-s-also-good-business

[29] HolonIQ. (n.d.). *Education in 2030 - The $10 Trillion dollar question*. Retrieved January 07, 2022 from https://www.holoniq.com/2030/

[30] Deloitte. (n.d.). *2021 Global health care outlook: Laying a foundation for the future*. Deloitte. Retrieved December 04, 2020 from https://www2.deloitte.com/content/dam/Deloitte/global/Documents/Life-Sciences-Health-Care/gx-lshc-2021-global-healthcare-infographic.pdf

GLOSSARY

InnovateHER: A woman who uses entrepreneurial skills and traits to create a positive impact while achieving a greater personal purpose.

Portrait of an InnovateHER: A combination of entrepreneurial personality traits and skills demonstrated by successful women who lead purpose-driven organizations. These specific traits and skills, derived from the EMP, show a unique entrepreneurial mindset that is more pronounced in women who choose to start new initiatives in the social-impact space.

Purpose-Driven Organizations: As defined by Pricewaterhouse-Coopers, it is "an organization that has purpose as its guidepost for decision-making—including the opportunities it decides to pursue and not pursue—to demonstrate commitment to responsible business leadership."

Entrepreneurial Mindset: "The constellation of motives, skills, and thought processes that distinguish entrepreneurs from non-entrepreneurs and that contribute to entrepreneurial success." For the purpose of this book, we have expanded the definition to apply to anyone building or scaling an organization using entrepreneurial traits and skills.

Entrepreneurial Traits: "The personality characteristics and motivations that have been found to distinguish entrepreneurs from non-entrepreneurs."

Entrepreneurial Skills: "The cognitive and behavioral skills critical to entrepreneurial success."

InhibitHER: These are internal traits and skills or external challenges that hold you back from success. These are the barriers that InnovateHERs must overcome along their path to the top.

ActivateHER: The key lessons and takeaways learned from overcoming InhibitHERs that fuel success.

APPENDIX A

InnovateHER Photos and Bios

Ana Hidalgo

Ana Hidalgo, founder of LAB XXI and ReinventED Schools, is passionate about using innovative education practices to drive social change throughout Latin America. Prior to founding her companies, she served as the Advisor in Foreign Affairs to the Mayor of Quito, Ecuador, and as a Graduate Fellow in the Executive Office of Education of Massachusetts. She has had the opportunity to represent Ecuador in the world's most important youth conference, One Young World, and she has spoken at seminars at the national and international levels.

Education Degrees and Institutions

BA, Foreign Affairs and Anthropology, University of Virginia
EdM, Harvard University

Anjlee Prakash

Anjlee Prakash is the founder and chairperson of the Learning Links Foundation. With a PhD in education and 30 years of experience as a techno-pedagogue, Dr. Anjlee Prakash has built one of India's most successful, tech-integrated education nonprofits. In addition to her work at Learning Links, she has held several other positions of responsibility in the academic, nongovernment, and corporate bodies. Her personal mission is to enhance the education ecosystem to make lifelong learning possible for every student.

Education Degrees and Institutions

MA, Agra University
EdM, Agra University
PhD, Education, Agra University
Certificate, Strategic Perspectives in Non-Profit Management,
    Harvard University
Certificate, Value Creation, INSEAD

Carol Ann Waugh

Carol Ann Waugh is an entrepreneur and artist. At 34 years old, Waugh quit her job as an executive for Progressive Grocer to start her own publishing company. After successfully growing the company, she sold it to R.R. Bowker. While serving as an industry consultant, she started another publishing firm that she sold to the Software & Information Industry Association. Today, she is a commissioned artist who lectures, teaches, and writes books.

Education Degrees and Institutions

BS, New York University
MBA, Pace University

Elissa Freiha

Elissa Freiha is an entrepreneur, investor, executive producer, public speaker, women's rights advocate, and founder of Womena, a digital media company that creates compelling female-focused content in the MENA region. As a prominent speaker on women's involvement in entrepreneurship and an active angel investor with over 30 investments between North America and MENA, Elissa has been frequently recognized in various media outlets, appearing on BBC's 30under30 series; Forbes Middle East's "50 Business Leaders Inspiring The UAE"; Arabian Business's "100 World's Most Influential Arabs," "100 Most Powerful Arab Women," and "100 Most Influential Arabs under 40"; One Young World's "Entrepreneur of the Year 2019"; and Forbes Middle East's "100 Power Business Women 2020"—as well as being named one of the 10 people who will shape the region over the next decade by *Esquire Magazine*. Prior to co-founding WOMENA, Elissa worked in marketing, sales, and events in entertainment and media. She holds a Bachelor of Arts in Global Communications from the American University of Paris, the city in which she was born and raised. She is an Emirati of Lebanese and American descent.

Education Degrees and Institutions

BA, Global Communications, American University of Paris
Public Relations, Communication Arts, Theology, Saint Louis University
Executive Education, Venture Capital, University of California, Berkeley

Jamie Candee

Jamie Candee serves as President, CEO, and Board Director of Edmentum, a global education leader that delivers research-based digital curriculum, assessments for learning, and quality educational consulting. In addition to her role as CEO, Jamie founded Edmentum's We Can Learn Foundation, which founded a school in the Nakivale Refugee Settlement in Uganda that has provided support to more than 10,000 children. Jamie also serves on the Board of Trustees for Visitation School and is Board of Directors for Project Success and Learning Tree International. In 2021, Jamie was recognized as the Ernst & Young Entrepreneur of The Year 2021 Heartland award winner.

Education Degrees and Institutions

BS, University of Wisconsin
MBA, Bethel University

Jane Kubasik

Jane Kubasik is the founder and former chair of the 114th Partnership. Since 2001, Kubasik has led multiple national and regional educator-employer collaborations designed to prepare and inspire students on the path toward professional readiness. Her groundbreaking approach is featured in numerous education and business publications, including a 2009 Harvard Business School case study, "Leading for Equity," and a 2014 University of Phoenix report, "Investment Criteria for STEM Education: What Counts for Excellence in STEM Programs?"

Education Degrees and Institutions

BS, Accounting, University of Maryland

Jennifer Ferrari

Jennifer Ferrari is the president and CEO of the Education Research and Development Institute (ERDI), an organization that convenes educational thought leaders to collaboratively shape, influence, and inform the development of PK–12 education products and services. Prior to joining ERDI, Jennifer spent 25 years in the field of public education as a middle school teacher, assistant principal, principal, assistant superintendent, and chief schools officer in Chicagoland. Her areas of expertise include leadership development, change management, strategic planning, curriculum and instruction, personalized learning, and dual language education.

Education Degrees and Institutions

BA, Political Science, Education, Lake Forest College
MA, Education, Curriculum and Instruction, National-Louis University
EdD, Administration and Supervision, Loyola University

Joysy John

Joysy John is a software engineer, EdTech entrepreneur and global speaker. Joysy is in the Financial Times Top 100 Most Influential BAME leaders in UK Tech. She was appointed by the Department of Education to the EdTech Leadership Group and by the Welsh Government to the expert panel on Schooling Reimagined. She left her banking career in 2012 to change education after spending a decade working across Singapore, US, and UK. She is the former CEO of 01 Founders, tuition-free coding schools with a job-guarantee to improve diversity in tech. Joysy is passionate about education, entrepreneurship, and women's empowerment. Previously she was the Director of Education at Nesta, UK's innovation foundation and Chief Industry Officer of Ada, the National College for Digital Skills.

Education Degrees and Institutions

BS, Computer Engineering, Nanyang Technological University
MBA, London Business School

Katie Fang

Katie Fang is the Founder and CEO of SchooLinks, an education technology company that offers advanced college and career planning solutions. As of 2021, SchooLinks is a venture-backed series and a startup headquartered in Austin, TX. Fang was named Forbes "Top 30 under 30," Top Texan under 30, the Young Woman to Watch, and has been featured on the cover of *Austin Woman Magazine*.

Education Degrees and Institutions

BA, Commerce, Finance, The University of British Columbia

Krishanti O'Mara Vignarajah

Krishanti (Krish) is the President and CEO of Lutheran Immigration and Refugee Service (LIRS). She previously served in the Obama White House as Policy Director for First Lady Michelle Obama and at the State Department as Senior Advisor under Secretaries of State Hillary Clinton and John Kerry. Before joining the White House, Krish practiced law at Jenner & Block in Washington, DC, clerked for Chief Judge Michael Boudin on the U.S. Court of Appeals for the First Circuit, and taught at Georgetown University as an adjunct. She holds a BS in Molecular Biology and an MA in Political Science from Yale College, a JD from Yale Law School, and an MPhil in International Relations from Oxford University (Marshall Scholarship). Krish has been recognized as one of *The Daily Record's* Top 50 Influential Marylanders, Top 100 Women, and Most Admired CEOs, as well as a 2021 Women to Watch by the *Baltimore Sun.*

Education Degrees and Institutions

BS, Molecular, Cellular, & Developmental Biology, Yale University
MA, Political Science, Yale University
MPhil, International Relations, Oxford University
JD, Yale University

Lezli Baskerville

Lezli Baskerville, a justice attorney, currently serves as CEO of the National Association for Equal Opportunity in Higher Education (NAFEO). Prior to joining NAFEO, she served as National Legislative Counsel for the NAACP and as Appellate Counsel at the Lawyers Committee for Civil Rights Under Law. She led The Baskerville Group, a legal collective of 12 female attorneys who provided legal and government relations representation, advocacy, and diversity services to purpose-driven organizations, corporations, and government entities. After her tenure as CEO of The College Board's Washington Office & Government Relations Chief, she transitioned into the CEO role at NAFEO. She is the organization's first female CEO. Attorney Baskerville is recognized by STEMConnector as one of "100 Women Leaders in STEM"; by *Diverse Issues in Higher Education* as one of "25 Women Making a Difference"; by *AOL Black Voices* as one of the nation's "Top 10 Black Women in Higher Education"; and by *Ebony Magazine* for six consecutive years as one of America's Top 100 Most Influential Association Leaders. Baskerville is acknowledged in *The History Makers* as a distinguished lawmaker.

Education Degrees and Institutions

BA, American Studies, Journalism, and Communications,
  Douglass College - Rutgers University
JD, Howard University
Advanced Leadership Institute Fellow,
  Harvard University
Honorary Doctorate of Laws, Benedict
  College
Doctorate of Humane Letters, Shaw
  University
Presidential Medal of Honor, University of
  Maryland Eastern Shore

Lisa Hall

Ms. Hall currently serves as Impact Chair at Apollo Global Management where she is part of the leadership team for the firm's private equity impact platform and has responsibility for the impact management elements of the strategy. Prior to joining Apollo, Ms. Hall was a Professor of Practice and a Fellow at Georgetown University's Beeck Center for Social Impact and Innovation, where she led research focused on creating a more inclusive economy. She previously served as a Managing Director at Anthos Fund & Asset Management ("AFAM"), where she launched and oversaw the firm's impact investing portfolio. Prior to AFAM, Ms. Hall was President and CEO of Calvert Impact Capital.

Ms. Hall covered community development policy issues as a Senior Policy Advisor for the National Economic Council and has diverse civic leadership and non-profit board experience. She is a graduate of The Wharton School at University of Pennsylvania and earned her MBA from Harvard Business School. Ms. Hall currently serves on the boards of Community Development Trust and Habitat for Humanity International.

Education Degrees and Institutions

BS, Wharton School of Business, University of Pennsylvania
MBA, Harvard Business School

Lisa Schmucki

Lisa Schmucki is the founder and CEO of edWeb.net, a social network that helps educators and professionals working in the field of education to connect, collaborate, and break down the silos and traditional barriers in education. Since its founding in 2008, edWeb.net has become an award-winning professional learning network that serves a global community of 1 million educators. edWeb.net is a five-time winner of the prestigious SIIA CODiE Award. Lisa has more than 30 years of experience with publishing and media companies in marketing and product development.

Education Degrees and Institutions

BA, History, Princeton University
MS, Accounting, New York University

Maia Sharpley

Maia Sharpley recently co-founded Juvo Ventures as a Managing Partner. She was previously a Partner at Learn Capital, and now continues to support Learn as an Advisor. Maia is (also) a Founder of Innovation for Equity, a non-profit focused on disrupting the status quo and improving outcomes for Black learners of all ages. She serves as a board member to many portfolio companies spanning the globe across all education subsections including Eduvanz, Onramp, RideAlong, SchooLinks, New Campus, ION Learning, Talenya and previously Bloomboard. SoloLearn, and Smashcut among others.

Education Degrees and Institutions

BA, Political Science and International Relations, Trinity College
MBA, Corporate Strategy, International Business, University of
    Michigan
Fellow, Class 24, Kauffman Fellows

Margaret Huber

Margaret Huber is the former Canadian Chief of Protocol for the Department of Foreign Affairs. Her service in the Department of Foreign Affairs included serving as an Ambassador in Europe, Asia, and the Middle East as well as with multiple international organizations. She is a community leader and currently sits on the board of directors for several nonprofits and companies in Canada and the United States, and she is a 2014 Harvard Advanced Leadership Institute Fellow.

Education Degrees and Institutions

BA, McGill University
Harvard Business School Advanced Management Program, Institute of Corporate Directors, Advanced Leadership Institute Fellow, Harvard University

Mary Louise Cohen

Mary Louise Cohen, a founding partner of Phillips & Cohen LLP, has represented whistleblowers for more than 25 years in lawsuits brought to remedy fraud against the United States. In 2014, she co-founded Talent Beyond Boundaries (TBB), which opens skilled migration pathways for skilled refugees to move to job opportunities in a new country. Working with governments, refugee-serving organizations, the business community, and local communities, TBB is building a safe and legal pathway for displaced people to move for work and resume their careers so they can rebuild their lives with dignity.

Education Degrees and Institutions

BA, University of North Carolina
JD, Harvard Law School

Megan Harney

Megan Harney is the founder and CEO of MIDAS Education. A former classroom teacher, Megan's classroom experience led her to create her own software application, providing tools to build online activities and to view and track student performance analytics. She leveraged her understanding of the power and promise of software to develop the

comprehensive Massively Integrated Data Analytics System (MIDAS) platform, which facilitates the implementation of competency-based and individualized learning programs at scale.

Education Degrees and Institutions:

BA, English and American Literature & Language; Computer Science, Harvard University
EdM, Technology, Innovation, and Education, Harvard University

Monica Valrani

Monica Valrani is CEO of Ladybird Nurseries, based in Dubai. Dedicated to the pursuit of quality education for young children, Monica earned a diploma and graduated with distinction in Montessori Teaching before serving as a directress in Gulf Montessori Nursery. Her success as a teacher, combined with her entrepreneurial mindset, led her to acquire Dubai's Tiny Home Montessori Nursery, where she led its day-to-day operations and expanded the operation, which led to a merger with Ladybird Nurseries. Ladybird currently serves over 300 children and has three locations, including the first LEED Gold certified preschool in the Middle East.

Education Degrees and Institutions

Diploma, Hotel Management, Belair Education Centre
Diploma, Montessori Teaching, London Montessori Centre

Nisha Ligon

Nisha Ligon is the co-founder and CEO of Ubongo, Africa's leading edutainment company for children. More than 24 million kids across Africa learn with Ubongo's popular animated TV and radio programs, Akili and Me and Ubongo Kids. Nisha is a social entrepreneur with a background in media and science and has a passion for education. She is a 2017 WISE Award Laureate and 2021 Elevate Prize winner. Nisha has produced content for the BBC, the *Guardian*, online learning platforms, and an award-winning documentary, *Twiga Stars*.

Education Degrees and Institutions

BS, Yale University
MSc, Imperial College London

Pam Mayer

Pam Mayer is the founder of eMindset Academy, a training organization designed to teach practicing leaders how to add science to the art of innovation. She is also an adjunct coach and trainer for the Leadership Development Institute at Eckerd College. In the 1990s, Pam had a VP role at the Center for Creative Leadership (CCL), where she was responsible for open-enrollment and custom programs at the Greensboro, North Carolina site, as well as for providing oversight of CCL's worldwide licensee network.

Education Degrees and Institutions

BA, Psychology, Old Dominion University
MA, Counseling, Pennsylvania State University
PhD, Educational Psychology, University of South Florida

Patricia Scanlon

Dr. Patricia Scanlon is the Founder and Executive Chair of SoapBox Labs, the world's leading provider of proprietary voice technology for children. Dr. Scanlon holds a PhD and 25 years' experience working in software engineering, Speech Recognition and Artificial Intelligence, including at Bell Labs and IBM. An acclaimed TEDx speaker, in 2018, Dr. Scanlon was named one of Forbes "Top 50 Women in Tech" globally. In 2020, she was ranked sixth of 17 global "Visionaries in Voice" by the industry-leading publication Voicebot.ai. She is the author of peer reviewed academic publications, holds five granted patents and is a contributing author for TechCrunch and TheNextWeb. Inspired by her oldest child and her background as a speech engineer, Dr. Scanlon founded SoapBox Labs in 2013 to redefine how children interact with technology using their voices.

Education Degrees and Institutions:

BS, Engineering, Technological University Dublin
PhD, Speech Recognition and Artificial Intelligence, University
    College Dublin

Rebecca Winthrop

Rebecca Winthrop is a senior fellow and co-director of the Center for Universal Education at the Brookings Institution. Her research focuses on education globally, with special attention to the skills young people need to thrive in work, life, and as constructive citizens. Dr. Winthrop works to promote quality and relevant education, including exploring how education innovations can leapfrog progress, particularly for the most marginalized youth. She advises governments, international institutions, foundations, civil society organizations, and corporations on education issues. She currently serves as a board member and advisor for a number of global education organizations and lectures at Georgetown University.

Education Degrees and Institutions

BA, Political Science and Dance Politics, Swarthmore College
MA, International Affairs, Columbia University
PhD, Education, Columbia University

Sabari Raja

Sabari Raja is the co-founder and CEO of Nepris, one of the fastest growing EdTech companies in the United States. Nepris is a cloud-based platform connecting industry and education to inspire students through real world connection and career exposure. Raja has worked in education technology for 18 years as the lead for product and content strategy, business development, publisher relations, and emerging market growth strategies. She serves on the board of directors for Friends of Texas Public Schools (FOTPS), Workforce Solutions Capital Area, and Texas Girls Collaborative.

Education Degrees and Institutions

BS, Engineering, Electronics and Communications, Bharathiar
    University
MS, Computer Science, Louisiana State University
MS, System Science, Louisiana State University
MBA, Business Administration, Southern Methodist University

Sherrie Westin

Sherrie Westin is the President of Sesame Workshop, the nonprofit organization behind *Sesame Street*. Prior to joining the Workshop, Westin held positions in the public, private, and nonprofit sectors, as well as media. She served as Assistant to the President in the first Bush White House and a senior executive at ABC News, *U.S. News & World Report*, and the ABC Television Network. She has been recognized as a "Leading Global Thinker" by *Foreign Policy Magazine*, one of *Fast Company*'s "100 Most Creative People in Business," and has received the Smithsonian's American Ingenuity Award.

Education Degrees and Institutions

BA, University of Virginia
Honorary Doctorate, Concordia College

Silver McDonald

Silver McDonald is Vice President of Growth at Hazel Health. At Hazel Health, she leads a team that works with schools to extend equitable physical and mental health services to all children and especially to those that have historically been underserved. Throughout her career, she has helped small startups grow to become publicly traded companies and more recently served as the General Manger of LEGO Education in North America, serving on the global LEGO Education leadership team. Silver McDonald has been an executive in the education and technology industries for more than 20 years.

Education Degrees and Institutions

BA, Technical and Professional Writing, San Francisco State University
MBA, Northwestern University
Certificate, Sustainability Strategies and Renewable Energies, Presidio
    Graduate School

Vicky Colbert

Laureate of the 2017 edition of the Yidan Prize for Education Development and 2013 WISE Prize for Education Laureate, Vicky Colbert is the founder and director of Fundación Escuela Nueva. She is co-creator of the worldwide renowned Escuela Nueva model and was its first National Coordinator. Colbert has pioneered, expanded, and sustained this educational innovation from many organizational spheres: as Vice Minister of Education of Colombia, UNICEF's Education Advisor for LAC, and now from Fundación Escuela Nueva (FEN), which she founded to ensure its quality, sustainability, and innovation in education.

Education Degrees and Institutions

BA, Sociology, Javeriana University
MA, Social Foundation of Education and Sociology of Education, Stanford University

Zoë Timms

Zoë Timms is the Founder and Executive Director of Women's Education Project (WEP), which she formed while living in India, for young women to become knowledgeable, confident, responsible leaders prepared to pursue their ambitions with an expanded awareness of life's opportunities. While building WEP, Zoë learned the South Indian languages Tamil and Telugu, both of which she speaks with great confidence but little accuracy. Using her grassroots experience and the vast knowledge and support of WEP Directors, Zoë has developed WEP's locally sourced, holistic curricula: I Am a Leader and the Leadership Academy. Zoë lives in Brooklyn with her husband, two children, and cat.

Education Degrees and Institutions

BA, History, University of Wisconsin

APPENDIX B

Interview Questions

1. Do you consider yourself to be an entrepreneur? Why?
2. Of the following personality traits, do you think ONE trait is the most important for an entrepreneur to possess and/or nurture? Why?
   a. Independence
   b. Preference for limited structure
   c. Nonconformity
   d. Risk-taking
   e. Action oriented
   f. Passion
   g. Need to achieve
3. Which of the following skills do you feel entrepreneurs should learn and nurture? Why? (You can choose more than one.)
   a. Future focus
   b. Idea generation
   c. Execution
   d. Self-confidence
   e. Optimism
   f. Persistence
   g. Interpersonal sensitivity
4. Do you believe that traits and skills necessary to be a successful entrepreneur are innate to an individual, or do you believe they can be learned?
5. Do you feel you've encountered barriers as a woman entrepreneur that would not have been encountered by your male counterparts? Give some examples.

6. What is the biggest challenge entrepreneurs—men or women—face in moving their ideas from concept to reality?

7. How do you reconcile risk-tolerance with security and work-life balance?

8. Do you think entrepreneurship is moving in the direction of dual-impact goals, i.e., products/services should "do good" and "produce capital/do well?"

Leadership-Related Questions

1. Did you have a mentor or mentors who taught you how to nurture your leadership or entrepreneurial skills? If so, who and how did she/he/they impact you?

2. Have you mentored other entrepreneurs? If so, what is the advice you have given? Have they been successful? How do you define success?

3. As a woman, do you feel you have a different definition of success as an entrepreneur compared to men?

4. Do you feel that women have different leadership skills than men?

5. Do you feel that women have to be more purposeful/mindful/strategic in building a path to leadership?

6. It is often said that an entrepreneur is not necessarily a great leader or CEO. Do you think this is true? What skills do entrepreneurs need to acquire in order to be true leaders?

APPENDIX C

Entrepreneurial Mindset Profile® Definitions and EMP Self-Assessment from Penn GSE

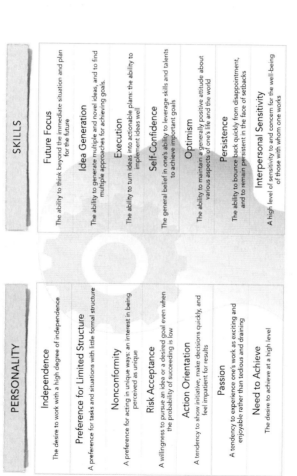

Entrepreneurial Mindset Profile® (EMP) Scale Definitions

SKILLS

Future Focus
The ability to think beyond the immediate situation and plan for the future

Idea Generation
The ability to generate multiple and novel ideas, and to find multiple approaches for achieving goals.

Execution
The ability to turn ideas into actionable plans: the ability to implement ideas well

Self-Confidence
The general belief in one's ability to leverage skills and talents to achieve important goals

Optimism
The ability to maintain a generally positive attitude about various aspects of one's life and the world

Persistence
The ability to bounce back quickly from disappointment, and to remain persistent in the face of setbacks

Interpersonal Sensitivity
A high level of sensitivity to and concern for the well-being of those with whom one works

PERSONALITY

Independence
The desire to work with a high degree of independence

Preference for Limited Structure
A preference for tasks and situations with little formal structure

Nonconformity
A preference for acting in unique ways: an interest in being perceived as unique

Risk Acceptance
A willingness to pursue an idea or a desired goal even when the probability of succeeding is low

Action Orientation
A tendency to show initiative, make decisions quickly, and feel impatient for results

Passion
A tendency to experience one's work as exciting and enjoyable rather than tedious and draining

Need to Achieve
The desire to achieve at a high level

Credit: Entrepreneurial Mindset Profile® (EMP) developed by Leadership Development Institute at Eckerd College (LDI)

Global Education Entrepreneurship+ Innovation

ENTREPRENEURIAL MINDSET SELF-ASSESSMENT

An Entrepreneurial Mindset is a collection of attitudes, beliefs, traits and skills that enable one to view uncertainty as an opportunity.

1. Which of the below are <u>your</u> greatest strengths?
(Select one Personality and one Skill in column 1)

PERSONALITY	1	2	SKILLS	1	2
Independence			Future Focus		
Preference for Limited Structure			Idea Generation		
Nonconformity			Execution		
Risk-Taking			Self-Confidence		
Action Orientation			Optimism		
Passion			Persistence		
Need to Achieve			Interpersonal Sensitivity		

2. Which of the above are <u>your</u> greatest areas for improvement?
(Select one Personality and one Skill in column 2)

3. Which of the below are <u>your team's</u> greatest strengths?
(Select up to two in each category on column 3)

PERSONALITY	3	4	SKILLS	3	4
Independence			Future Focus		
Preference for Limited Structure			Idea Generation		
Nonconformity			Execution		
Risk-Taking			Self-Confidence		
Action Orientation			Optimism		
Passion			Persistence		
Need to Achieve			Interpersonal Sensitivity		

4. Which of the above are <u>your team's</u> greatest areas for improvement?
(Select up to two in each category on column 4)

WHY?
(Please write a response for each question.)

Adapted from Eckerd College's Entrepreneurial Mindset Profile® (EMP) + NFTE's EMI

Global Education Entrepreneurship+Innovation

Graduate School of Education
PennGSE

APPENDIX D

Demographics

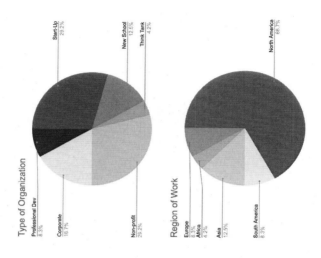

Type of Organization

Start-Up 29.2%
New School 12.5%
Think Tank 4.2%
Professional Dev 8.3%
Corporate 16.7%
Non-profit 29.2%

Region of Work

North America 66.7%
Europe 8.3%
Africa 4.2%
Asia 12.5%
South America 8.3%

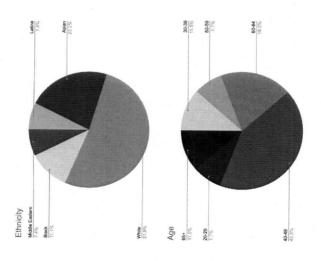

Ethnicity

Latina 7.4%
Asian 22.2%
Middle Eastern 7.4%
Black 11.1%
White 51.9%

Age

30-39 11.5%
50-59 7.7%
60-64 19.2%
65+ 11.5%
20-29 7.7%
40-49 42.3%

ABOUT THE AUTHORS

Barbara Kurshan

Barbara "Bobbi" Kurshan is the President of Educorp Consultants Corporation and is the Senior Innovation Advisor at the Graduate School of Education, Education Entrepreneurship Program at the University of Pennsylvania. An education industry entrepreneur, Dr. Kurshan has more than 40 years of experience in education as a researcher, entrepreneur, developer, investor, and executive. She developed the first children's software products for Microsoft, as well as award-winning products for McGraw-Hill and Apple. She has authored several books and numerous articles on education, entrepreneurship, and innovation. She received the prestigious King Bahrain UNESCO Prize, the WISE Prize and was selected as one of the 2019 Most Influential Corporate Board Directors.

Kathy Hurley

A former senior executive for educational publishing and technology companies, including IBM and Pearson, Kathy Hurley is a senior advisor to EdTech companies, education associations, and school superintendent networks. She was selected as a Fellow of the Advanced Leadership Initiative at Harvard University and subsequently co-founded the global nonprofit organization Girls Thinking Global, which has since merged with the Women's Education Project, where she serves on the board of directors.

In 2004 she was inducted into the Association of Educational Publishers' Hall of Fame and in 2019 received the prestigious Lifetime Achievement Award in Education Technology from the Software &

Information Industry Association. She received the 2022 Founders Award from NCTET, the inaugural Distinctive Mentor Award from ERDI, and the Lifetime Achievement Award from ALAS. She is co-editor of *Real Women, Real Leaders: Surviving and Succeeding in the Business World* (Wiley).

LET'S STAY IN TOUCH

Website: www.innovateHERs.org
Twitter: @innovate_HERs
Instagram: @innovatehers
Facebook: InnovateHERs Community
LinkedIn: InnovateHERs Community

Contact: info@innovateHERs.org

Made in United States
North Haven, CT
14 March 2023

34053661R00139